Ivan Turgenev

Twayne's World Authors Series

Russian Literature

Charles A. Moser, Editor

George Washington University

TWAS 776

Ivan Turgenev
(1818-1883)

Ivan Turgenev

By A. V. Knowles

University of Liverpool

Twayne Publishers
A Division of G. K. Hall & Co. • *Boston*

Ivan Turgenev
A. V. Knowles

Copyright 1988 by G. K. Hall & Co.
All rights reserved.
Published by Twayne Publishers
A Division of G. K. Hall & Co.
70 Lincoln Street
Boston, Massachusetts 02111

Copyediting supervised by Barbara Sutton.
Book production by Janet Zietowski.
Book design by Barbara Anderson.

Typeset in 11 pt. Garamond
by Compositors Typesetters, Cedar Rapids, Iowa.

Printed on permanent/durable acid-free paper
and bound in the United States of America.

Library of Congress Cataloging-in-Publication Data
Knowles, A. V. (Anthony Vere)
  Ivan Turgenev.

  (Twayne's world authors series; TWAS 776. Russian
literature)
  Bibliography: p.
  Includes index.
  1. Turgenev, Ivan Sergeevich, 1818-1883—Criticism
and interpretation.   I. Title.   II. Series.
PG3443.K6   1988   891.73'3   88-11220
ISBN 0-8057-8241-9 (alk. paper)

Contents

About the Author

A. V. Knowles earned his bachelor's degree in Slavonic Studies at the University of Nottingham, and after a year's study at the Leningrad State University he returned to Nottingham, where he received his master's degree in Russian history in 1964 for a thesis on the activities of the Populist Chaykovsky Circle in St. Petersburg in the early 1870s. He was then appointed to the staff of the University of Liverpool, where he is currently senior lecturer in Russian.

Knowles's principal academic interests are the history of Russian literature in the nineteenth century and Russian history during the reigns of Peter I and Catherine II. He is the author of a number of articles and reviews on Russian literature, history, and drama; the coauthor of *Angleščina za Vsakogar* (1962, 1965); and the editor of *How Robinson was Created, and Other Stories* by I. Il'f and E. Petrov (1968), *Tolstoy: The Critical Heritage* (1978), and *Turgenev's Letters* (1983).

Preface

In this study I have tried to do justice to Ivan Turgenev, whose extensive writings appeared over nearly fifty years and included poetry, plays, short stories, and novels. I could not discuss his oeuvre nor pay due respect to the generally helpful criticism it has evoked, but I have attempted to assess the more interesting and lasting of his writings and to show why—although he may strike the modern reader as a little old-fashioned—Turgenev was called Russia's greatest living writer in 1879 and is still well worth reading today.

After an introductory chapter that surveys Turgenev's generally uneventful life and sets his fiction in its historical context, I examine his early attempts at composing poetry, short stories, and plays in order to highlight the themes, ideas, characters, and methods that he later employed with greater success and conviction. The bulk of the study concerns *A Sportsman's Sketches*, the work that first made Turgenev famous, his best-known short stories, and his struggles with the difficulties of writing novels, as well as the ways in which he attempted to reflect what he considered the most salient factors of Russia's contemporary historical development. The final chapter surveys his literary career and offers a number of conclusions.

Although it is difficult to be definitive about Turgenev as man or writer—for example, did he have any precise or coherent opinions on writing, life, or Russia? was he best at portraiture and the miniature? did he overreach himself in writing novels? was he a master of a certain type of short story? was he a reliable chronicler of his times? did a fear of illness and a constant awareness of death cloud his judgment? were his personal experiences with women too bitter or unusual to allow him to view love positively?—I hope at least to provide some guidance on such questions, some pointers and encouragement to those reading his work for the first time.

All translations from Turgenev's works or correspondence are my own, unless otherwise acknowledged.

I am grateful to Professor Charles Moser, the editor of this series, for suggesting that I prepare this volume and for his help during its completion. I would especially like to thank Sheila Armer for typing my manuscript with patience, cheerfulness, and accuracy, and for her kindness and gentle encouragement when other, less joyful, matters threatened its completion.

A. V. Knowles

University of Liverpool

Chronology

1863   Takes up residence in Baden-Baden, near the Viardots. Investigated by Senate for political connections with Herzen and Ogarev in London.

1864   Cleared of suspicion by Senate. Breaks with Herzen.

1865   Daughter marries.

1867   *Smoke*. Quarrels with Dostoyevski.

1870   "King Lear of the Steppes."

1871   Returns to live in Paris (until his death). Friendships with Flaubert, George Sand, and Zola.

1872   "Torrents of Spring."

1877   *Virgin Soil*.

1878   Reconciliation with Tolstoy.

1879   Visits Russia; enthusiastic reception from the young. Brother dies. Awarded honorary doctor of civil law by Oxford University; first meeting with the actress Marya Savina.

1880   Pushkin celebrations in Moscow; reconciliation with Dostoyevski.

1882   Daughter leaves husband. Sells his treasured collection of paintings to support her and her children.

1883   Operation to remove malignant tumor from abdomen. 3 September, dies at Bougival near Paris from cancer of the spine; 27 September, buried at the Volkovo cemetery in St. Petersburg.

Chapter One
Biographical Sketch

Childhood and Education

Ivan Sergeevich Turgenev was born at noon on 28 October 1818 in his parents' home in Orel in the heart of European Russia, some 200 miles south of Moscow. He was baptized three days later.

His father, Sergey Nikolaevich, was from the minor gentry. Decorated for bravery at the Battle of Borodino in 1812, he attained the rank of lieutenant-colonel in the cavalry before retiring voluntarily in 1821. Five years before, at twenty-three, he had married the twenty-nine-year-old Varvara Petrovna Lutovinova, an attractive and extremely wealthy landowner. While his reasons for marriage were almost certainly mercenary, she by all accounts married for love. Although concerned about his sons' education and, unusually for his class and times, insisting that they spend many hours perfecting their knowledge of the Russian language, Turgenev's father was more interested in outside pursuits, especially in women other than his wife. She was left to bring up their two sons (a third died in adolescence) and run their various estates, where she gained a reputation for brutality toward her serfs, a fact that made a lasting impression upon the young Ivan. Turgenev was to leave a vivid description of his parents' strained relationship in his story "Pervaya lyubov'" ("First Love").

When he was seventeen Turgenev wrote that he had been an ugly and spoilt child,[1] although on another occasion he said that his upbringing was spartan in the extreme and that he was often beaten for no apparent reason.[2] Despite these conflicting statements, there is little reason to suppose that his early years were anything but generally happy.

Of Turgenev's early reading little is known, but he later recalled that in his childhood he had been a voracious and indiscriminate reader—the classics, the fables of Dmitriev and Krylov, and the poetry of Kheraskov.[3] His father's library at the main estate at Spasskoe, which Turgenev described in "Faust" and which he eventually inherited, contained works by eighteenth- and early nineteenth-century Russian writers, notably Sumarokov, Derzhavin, Fonvizin, and Karamzin. The early chapters of Pushkin's *Eugene Onegin* were

1

certainly in the library, but we do not know whether Turgenev read them as a boy or what he then thought of Pushkin's poetry, which was to have a lasting influence on him throughout his life.

Turgenev was educated first at home, where a succession of tutors taught him arithmetic, algebra, geometry, physics, history, geography, and languages. Then, after short periods at private boarding schools, he was admitted to the faculty of literature at Moscow University at the age of fifteen. At this period Moscow University was undoubtedly the intellectual center of Russia, but although Turgenev spent a year there, there is no evidence to suggest that he became acquainted at the time with any of his older contemporaries such as the writers and thinkers Nikolay Stankevich, Alexander Herzen, and Nikolay Ogarev, the poet Mikhail Lermontov, the novelist Ivan Goncharov, or Russia's first original and influential literary critic, Vissarion Belinsky. In the early summer of 1834 Turgenev moved to St. Petersburg in order to be with his father and brother, enrolling at the university there in the faculty of history and philology where he had the dubious privilege of attending lectures given by Gogol, not the most notable professor of world history. In October his father died. Shortly before this he had started work on his first literary effort, a dramatic poem, *Steno*, based on and imitating Byron's *Manfred*. After graduating at the second attempt in 1837, he returned with his widowed mother to Spasskoe, where he passed his time pleasantly enough, indulging in his lifelong passion for hunting and shooting, observing the peasant life he was later to portray so sympathetically in *Zapiski okhotnika* (*A Sportsman's Sketches*), and getting to know the environment that was to be the setting of much of his writing.

Turgenev spent the years 1838 to 1841 mainly abroad. He studied at the University of Berlin, where for a short time he shared a flat with the future anarchist Mikhail Bakunin, whom he was to portray, partly, as the eponymous Rudin, and became infected, as did most of his generation, with German romantic philosophy. He later explained that his decision to go to Germany was influenced by his growing hatred of serfdom. That way of life, he wrote, and his native surroundings did not represent anything that could detain him. On the contrary, nearly everything he saw aroused in him feelings of shame and indignation, even of revulsion. Serfdom became an enemy from which he had to get away so that he could attack it more powerfully from a distance. As confirmation he added that he could never have written any of *A Sportsman's Sketches* had he remained in Russia. He therefore plunged, as he put it, into the German sea; when he came to the surface he was a "Westernizer" and remained such ever after.[4]

These years also saw Turgenev acquainting himself more with Western

Europe, especially Italy, where, as he told his friend Timofey Granovsky, his "eyes were first opened to the beauties of art." On his return to Russia he settled again at Spasskoe, became the father of an illegitimate daughter, Paulinette, of whom he was never fond, and took to writing poetry.

The Start of a Literary Career

Turgenev's first venture into literature had been his poem *Steno* of 1834. Despite adverse, and quite justified criticism, he persevered with various verse genres, although he later wrote that he never cared for his own poetry. Nonetheless, he became a regular contributor to the literary journal *Otechestvennye zapiski* (*Fatherland Notes*). He entered the civil service in the Ministry of the Interior, wrote an interesting memorandum on serfdom, and in 1843 published the first work to establish his reputation as a writer, a verse romance entitled *Parasha*. It was the success, largely ensured by Belinsky's enthusiastic review, of this "story in verse" that convinced him that his future lay in writing.

The year 1843 was also important for Turgenev in another respect: it marked the beginning of the greatest friendship of his life. Pauline Viardot, one of the most celebrated opera singers of the time, wife of the critic and art historian Louis Viardot, came on tour to Moscow and captivated the young Turgenev. Thus began a very long-lasting and stable relationship. For forty years, to the day of his death, Turgenev lived as near the Viardots as he could. His lifelong devotion, probably platonic, to Pauline is almost certainly the reason why he never married and was the cause, according to many of his contemporaries, of his living so rarely in Russia.

Early in 1845 Turgenev resigned from the civil service on the pretext of poor eyesight and applied for his passport in order to join Pauline in France. He returned to Russia later that year and became involved in the rebirth of the journal originally founded by Pushkin, *Sovremennik* (*Contemporary*). The edition of January 1847 contained nine of his poems and the short story "Khor and Kalinych," which the journal's coeditor, Ivan Panaev, subtitled "From a Sportsman's Sketches." Belinsky, despite his earlier praise for *Parasha*, rightly deduced that Turgenev's future lay with such stories and not with his poetry. But Turgenev, who was experimenting at the time with various literary genres, also tried his hand at writing plays, the most notable and enduring of which was *Mesyats v derevne* (*A Month in the Country*). Despite the critical acclaim accorded the series of pictures of peasant life known collectively as *A Sportsman's Sketches* and the success of the separately published "Mumu," Turgenev's most forthright indictment of serfdom, perhaps the work of this period of greatest importance for the history of nineteenth-century Russian literature is "Dnevnik lishnego cheloveka" ("The Diary of a Superfluous Man") written while he was abroad in 1849. The term "superfluous man," first given currency in this story, has long since become a cliché of Russian literary criticism as a label for basically positive heroes who find themselves out of place—socially, politically, and more importantly, psychologically—in contemporary society. They include such characters as Griboedov's Chatsky, Pushkin's Eugene Onegin, Lermontov's Demon and Pechorin, and Goncharov's Oblomov.

In the summer of 1850 Turgenev's mother died. As she left no will, Turgenev and his brother Nikolay had a number of difficulties over their inheritance. Once these were settled they shared their mother's various estates and properties and both became independent landowners. Although not as wealthy as he thought he would be, Turgenev was now reasonably financially secure. He might have grown as rich as his brother, who died a ruble millionaire, had he not proved incompetent, and little interested, in running his lands and been so unwise as to appoint as estate managers during his long absences abroad first his uncle, who seems to have spent most of the income on himself and his family, and then one N. Kishinsky, who proved dishonest.

At this point Turgenev did continue to write, although he was hardly prolific. There were three plays, the most successful of which, *Provintsialka* (*A Provincial Lady*) was staged in Moscow and St. Petersburg in 1851. But Turgenev had a poor opinion of himself as a dramatist and, becoming disheartened because the earlier *Nakhlebnik* (*A Poor Gentleman*) and *A Month in the Country* had been banned from performance by the censor, he ceased writing for the theater altogether. During this period he also composed a number of literary articles and reviews, notably one on Goethe's *Faust*, and some short stories, including "Andrey Kolosov," "Zhid" ("The Jew"), and his foray into the supernatural, "Tri portreta" ("Three Portraits").

Arrest and Exile

The period from 1850 to 1856 was the longest Turgenev ever spent again in Russia at a stretch, but this was not of his own choosing. In February 1852 Gogol died, and Turgenev submitted a short obituary to the St. Petersburg censor. Ever since the appearance of his play *The Inspector General* in 1836 Gogol had been regarded as the leading satirist of the reign of Nicholas I. After the publication of the novel *Dead Souls* in 1842 the authorities regarded him with increasing disfavor as someone bent only on slandering his motherland. Consequently they preferred his death to pass unnoticed and

Turgenev's obituary was therefore refused publication. He then submitted it in Moscow where (such were the vagaries of the censorship) it was passed and appeared in March 1852. When the czar learned the "facts" of the case, Turgenev was arrested. He spent a month in prison and was then exiled to Spasskoe. Turgenev never doubted that the real reason for his arrest was not the obituary alone but his reputation as a champion of the peasantry gained from *A Sportsman's Sketches*. Indeed, when a collection of them appeared as a book a few months later and rapidly sold out, the censor who passed them was summarily dismissed.

Turgenev said he found his eighteen-month exile rather tedious, although a reading of his letters from this time suggests otherwise. After continual applications he was permitted to return to St. Petersburg in November 1853, and entered the literary and social life of the capital with obvious enthusiasm. He met and became friends with a wide range of Russian literary figures, notably the editor and lyric poet Nikolay Nekrasov, the writers Ivan Goncharov and Leo Tolstoy, and perhaps the greatest memoirist of the nineteenth century in Russia, Pavel Annenkov. With each of the first three Turgenev was later seriously to disagree over various matters in disputes that became embarrassingly public, but Annenkov remained one of Turgenev's most faithful friends and confidants to the very end.

With the death of Nicholas I in 1855 and the conclusion of the Crimean War a year later, Turgenev received permission to go abroad, where he lived for the next few years. He took up residence near the Viardots in Paris, traveled to Germany, Italy, and England, and returned periodically to Russia. Although his relations with Pauline Viardot were not at their smoothest and his health and finances not at their best, he later wrote that this was probably the happiest time of his life.

A Literary Reputation Established

During the first half of the 1850s Turgenev made a conscious effort to find a different literary style for himself. Wishing to forget his early poetry, discarding the writing of plays, and saying that he could not go on producing stories from *A Sportsman's Sketches* forever, he thought that the novel might be the form best suited to him. Although he did not forsake writing shorter pieces—for instance "Zatish'e" ("A Quiet Spot"), "Dva priyatelya" ("Two Friends"), "Perepiska" ("A Correspondence"), "Yakov Pasynkov," and "Asya" all belong to these years—he was nonetheless certain that he could now be of more use to his country as a novelist. He began *Dva pokoleniya* (*Two Generations*), which he failed to finish, although a short chapter was published in

1859 as "Sobstvennaya gospodskaya kontora" ("The Privy Office"), and then
in the summer of 1855 started *Rudin*, which appeared the following year.
This was followed by *Dvoryanskoe gnezdo* (*Home of the Gentry*) in 1859,
Nakanune (*On the Eve*) in 1860, and *Ottsy i deti* (*Fathers and Sons*) in 1862.

The period from the accession of Alexander II in 1855 to the publication
of *Fathers and Sons* in 1862 marks the high point of Turgenev's success and
popularity in Russia. After the repressive thirty-year reign of Nicholas I, Russian educated society was producing ideas for reform and showing a clear enthusiasm for change. Turgenev found himself regarded as one of the leading
spokesmen for this new spirit. Already famous for his supposed denuncia-
tions of serfdom, his first three novels reflected many of the arguments going
on in Russia. *Rudin* was seen as praising the idealism of the older generation
without hiding its faults; *Home of the Gentry* depicted all that was best in the
old landowning class; and in *On the Eve* he attempted to portray a heroic
young girl of the new generation. All the leading critics of the day, whatever
their political or social persuasion, seemed to find in his novels support for
their own arguments. Turgenev was seen as writing about Russian life as it
was and choosing as his subject matter the most important problems of his
time; without romanticizing or philosophizing he had discovered that middle
course which his predecessors had failed to find; his graceful style was the
model of how such things should be done. Turgenev was always extremely
sensitive to his critics, and when it was pointed out that he had given Russian
literature a marvelous succession of heroines but had failed to present a convincing *Russian* hero—after all, Insarov in *On the Eve* was a Bulgarian—he
decided to make good this deficiency. In *Fathers and Sons* he wrote about his
young nihilist hero Bazarov with both affection and admiration and attempted, fairly he believed, to contrast him with the best of the older generation. But Turgenev was upset over the novel's reception. The outraged
radicals saw Bazarov as a grotesque caricature created simply to please the reactionaries. While it is true that a younger and more extreme section of the
radicals rejected this opinion, Turgenev never got over the initial response to
his novel, despite the equally strong support from other quarters. Embarrassed by the furor he had unwittingly created, he decided to abandon Russia
and Russian literature for good.

Life Abroad

In 1863 the Viardots decided to leave France. Pauline's voice was not what
it had been, and so she terminated her long connection with the Paris Opera
and limited her future performances to the smaller German centers and to re-

citals, while Louis was finding the repressive political atmosphere in France less and less to his taste. They had a villa built, on the outskirts of Baden-Baden in the Black Forest, which was soon to become a notable social and musical center. Both Clara Schumann, who soon made her home in the town, and Brahms, who followed her there, were frequent visitors, as was Wagner, whom Turgenev described as the founder of the school of "groaning in art."[5] In the summer of 1863 Turgenev also settled in Baden-Baden, where he rented the upper half of a large house for some five years until he moved into one he had built on land adjoining the Viardot villa. The early years in Baden-Baden were generally happy ones: the countryside was superb, the shooting excellent, and the company exciting. Even his chronic ill-health improved. He was also considerably cheered by managing to find a man he thought would be a suitable husband for his daughter Paulinette, who had been brought up in the main as part of the Viardot family. Sadly, he proved far from suitable, and when she finally left him with her young children a few years afterwards, Turgenev had to sell his collection of paintings to support them.

There were, however, other problems. Turgenev's finances were in disarray, for his estates in Russia were being mismanaged, and he had failed to claim the compensation due him under the Emancipation Act of 1861; there was a Senate inquiry into his supposed political activities; and his writings brought him a relatively small income. His habitual generosity to everyone did not help. He also fell out with two of his friends. Bakunin, a companion of his student days, had recently escaped from imprisonment in Russia and made his way to Western Europe. Despite Turgenev's opinion by then that Bakunin was a dangerous buffoon, Turgenev was instrumental in obtaining permission for Bakunin's wife to join him. Whatever gratitude Bakunin might have felt for Turgenev's help, their political views were by then so different that he blackened Turgenev's character at every opportunity. And many were pleased to believe him.

More far-reaching and instructive, though, was the break with Herzen. On a visit to London in 1861 Turgenev had long arguments with Herzen over the future of Russia, and in the following year Herzen published a series of articles in the form of open letters to a friend in his journal *Kolokol* (*Bell*), entitled *Ends and Beginnings*. The plan was for Turgenev to reply in similar fashion, but veiled warnings from the Russian authorities made him respond privately. Herzen restated his ideas on the theme that Western civilization had reached the end of its potential and was sinking into complacency. The only hope for progress lay with the ordinary Russian people, who had so far played little role in mankind's development but would, by avoiding the mistakes of Western Europe, in time have everything to offer. Turgenev replied that Russians and Europeans were basically the same creatures and that Russians would therefore have to follow the same path as Europe. It was no use believing in the uneducated and ignorant Russian people and filling them with a half-fermented Slavophile brew. If there was any hope it lay in the Russian *educated* class. Turgenev suggested that Herzen should stop his dreaming and look seriously at Western liberal ideas and practice. As the correspondence continued, the mutual bitterness intensified until Herzen published a scurrilous anecdote in the *Bell* about Turgenev. This was strenuously denied and Herzen was forced to print, if not exactly an apology, then at least a withdrawal of the insult. But relations between the two were not the same again until just before Herzen's death, when, Turgenev being the man he was, they were reconciled.

The time between the publication of *Fathers and Sons* in 1862 and the start of his next novel *Dym* (*Smoke*) at the end of 1864 shows very little literary activity from Turgenev. The short story "Prizraki" ("Ghosts") is extremely pessimistic about the future of mankind and was clearly influenced by Turgenev's shock at the reception of *Fathers and Sons*; the tale "Dovol'no" ("Enough") is a collection of memories about an unhappy past, and its overstated description of the depths of despair was one of the motivations behind Dostoyevski's cruel parody of Turgenev as the writer Karmazinov in *The Devils*; and finally a story of the supernatural, "Sobaka" ("The Dog").

Smoke seems to have been designed originally as a love story, but events in Russia after 1861 led Turgenev to attempt an analysis of what he saw as two important, and worrying, developments in Russia: the failure to implement the provisions of the Emancipation and the growth in radical activity. If Turgenev hoped that *Smoke* would be better received in Russia than *Fathers and Sons*, he was sadly disappointed. On its appearance in 1867 its strongly pro-Western and anti-Slavophile contents pleased hardly anyone. Perhaps typical of the general reaction was Dostoyevski's comment that Turgenev knew very little about what was taking place in Russia and really should be sent a telescope to help him see what was actually going on there. Indeed, Turgenev himself felt the justice of such remarks. Although he returned to Russia regularly during the last twenty or so years of his life, he remained only for short periods, and constantly worried that he was getting out of touch. Such a view might help explain why after *Smoke* his writings generally avoided contemporary problems, even though his last novel, *Nov'* (*Virgin Soil*) of 1877, attempted to describe the activities of the Russian populists of the 1870s. But most of his writing displayed an increasing nostalgia and deepening pessimism.

The Last Years

The happy and settled life in Baden-Baden came to an end. In the late fall of 1868 the Viardots moved to Karlsruhe, where there were wider possibilities for the education of their children, and Turgenev—who wrote that he found life without them frightening—soon followed. After visits to Paris and Weimar, Turgenev left for Russia in May 1870, while the Viardots returned to Baden-Baden. On his way back to join them Turgenev found himself in Berlin on the day the long-expected Franco-Prussian war broke out. His sympathies were firmly with the Prussians, though not so much from any love of them as from hatred for Napoleon III. Toward the end of 1870 the Viardots left for London with Turgenev soon in their wake. This period of upheaval in his life coincided with an increased literary output that culminated in one of his most characteristic stories, "Veshnie vody" ("The Torrents of Spring").

With the end of the war and the collapse of the Paris Commune, the Viardots and Turgenev returned to the French capital where Turgenev, despite his dislike for it, remained until the end of his life, passing the winters in Paris and the summers in Bougival, about an hour's drive away. He also made regular visits to Russia.

After the appearance of *Virgin Soil* in 1877 and its unfavorable reception, Turgenev frequently assured his correspondents that he had given up writing altogether, and apart from a few short stories and the *Senilia* or *Prose Poems* he in fact did not produce much. His interests turned to French politics, especially to the differences that became clear from the mid-seventies between the monarchical Patrice MacMahon, president of the Chamber of Deputies, and the various republican groupings within the majority. Turgenev's sympathies lay solidly with the republicans, especially with Léon Gambetta, and he was delighted when the elections of 1877 led to MacMahon's ouster. He was even more passionately interested in Russia's policy of protecting the Slav minorities living under Turkey's repressive rule in the Balkans and in the war that began in 1877. While his feelings of patriotism bore no trace at all of the widespread Pan-Slav sympathies in his homeland, he was shocked by the Turkish atrocities and saddened by the British government's opposition to Russian actions.[6]

For several years after the completion of *Virgin Soil* Turgenev returned to Russia annually. Two of these visits were particularly memorable. In February 1879 he was given a dinner at Moscow University where a select gathering hailed him as Russia's greatest living writer and he was reduced to tears. After all, he did not need to be reminded that both Tolstoy and Dostoyevski were still alive. But there was a further surprise in store. A week later he attended a public meeting of the Society of Lovers of Russian Literature in the largest lecture hall of Moscow University. To his utter amazement, delight, and, as he admitted, consternation, he was greeted by an ovation. All the abuse he felt he had suffered from the Russian public, especially its younger elements, over his novels seemed to have disappeared. That view was confirmed by the tumultuous reception he received from a thousand students a few days later at a reading he gave from A *Sportsman's Sketches.*

In 1880 Turgenev returned to Russia to help organize and participate in celebrations to honor Pushkin. His speech, albeit not one of his better pieces, was received coolly. Pushkin's genius, he said, lay in his ability to combine foreign and Russian influences and thereby create truly Russian art through a superb language. Pushkin was perhaps not a poet of world stature, but surely, Turgenev concluded, he would have become one had he not died so young. On the following day came the highlight of the proceedings, a speech by Turgenev's old enemy Dostoyevski. Dostoyevski praised Pushkin above all else for his Russianness and expressed the hope that the qualities within the Russian people would unite mankind. Despite his fundamental disagreement with such Slavophile sentiments, Turgenev, temporarily at least, forgave Dostoyevski for their political, and personal, antagonisms. The two writers embraced. However, Turgenev saw Dostoyevski's address as a victory for the chauvinistic and anti-Western tendency among his compatriots that he had opposed almost all his life.

Because he lived so long outside Russia, it is not surprising that Turgenev became the first Russian writer to be widely recognized in Western Europe. Translations of his books, especially into French and German, appeared with increasing frequency from the late 1860s onward. He was well known in French literary circles, being acquainted with Mérimée, George Sand, Maupassant, Zola, the Goncourts, and especially with Flaubert. And Henry James even included a section on Turgenev in a collection of essays on French authors. Foreigners were always impressed by Turgenev's charm and modesty and admired his talents as a writer; they seemed oblivious to faults of character that caused many of his compatriots to fall out with him. In 1879 this "gentle barbarian" was the first novelist ever to be honored by Oxford University with the award of an honorary doctorate.

The last few years of Turgenev's life were marked by frequent illness, a deepening sadness, and a feeling of resignation, all accompanied by a decline in his literary output. By the spring of 1882 he was seriously ill. None of the many doctors he consulted diagnosed his complaint accurately: they saw a sort of angina instead of the actual cancer of the spine. After an extremely unpleasant operation to remove a tumor from his abdomen in early 1883, his health rapidly declined, and, after one or two brief respites from the increasingly unbearable pain, he died on 3 September. Pauline Viardot was with him to the very end. His body was taken back to St. Petersburg, and in the Volkovo Cemetery he was buried not far from Belinsky, the man who first recognized his literary talents.

Epilogue

From the perspective of a hundred years' time, Turgenev's life, like that of many other nineteenth-century writers, appears generally uneventful. He might have fallen into a bear-pit in Switzerland when a little boy, escaped drowning on a burning steamer on the way to Germany as a young man, or been in Paris at the time of the 1848 revolution and in Germany during the Franco-Prussian War. He might have lived through momentous times in Russia's history: the reign of Nicholas I, the Crimean War, the emancipation of the peasants, the Populist movement of the seventies, and the assassination of Alexander II. Yet he rarely chose to participate; he preferred to observe. To his more forthright Russian contemporaries he appeared variously shallow, vain, arrogant, vacillating, and superficial, yet to many others he was a kind, polite, charming, considerate, and modest man, although rather lazy, forgetful, and weak-willed. He often lacked self-confidence as both a man and a writer. He was a hypochondriac and in later life rather melancholy and pessimistic. Perhaps, as Pauline Viardot thought, he really was the saddest of men. He had little regard for money, although he got upset when it was in short supply and was a little envious of his elder brother's financial acumen and great wealth, but he was generous to almost everyone. He enjoyed women's company greatly but their bodies rarely. He was a poor father but a splendid "uncle." He was an agnostic and a lover of personal freedom. Albeit extremely interested in politics, he was never politically active, and disliked those who were. Although he always said he hated all strong convictions, he held firmly to certain beliefs all his life. He desired moderation in all things; he had a deep aversion to fanaticism and all "systems," whether social, political, or moral. He preferred gradualism to revolution; a liberal perhaps, he believed fervently in reforms from above. When in March 1875 Countess Marya Milyutina asked him to help her schoolboy son with an essay on "Turgenev's Philosophy of Life," he was bemused at the sort of thing school teachers were inflicting upon their pupils and reluctantly replied that he was first and foremost a realist; more than anything he was interested in human

beings; he was indifferent to everything supernatural, and had no faith whatsoever in any absolutes or orthodoxies. Most of all he loved freedom.

He also loved chess, painting, music, literature, nature, shooting, and
dogs. He loved children too—but other people's.

On the personal level, Turgenev liked a quiet life in congenial company.
When life was not quiet or the company not congenial, he would retreat into
illness. He was fond of saying that his entire biography lay in his books, and
while that is clearly not the whole story, it is at bottom true. It is for his writings and not for his life that he will be remembered.

Chapter Two
The Start of a Literary Career
Poetry

Turgenev's poetry belongs largely to the 1840s, when he was still a young man serving what might be called his literary apprenticeship. He left a handful of narrative poems and about one hundred shorter, mainly lyrical, works. Most of them owe a debt to Pushkin in particular and to the romanticism popular in Russia at the time. Later in life Turgenev was disparaging about them all, and compared to his prose works they are indeed of minor interest. Yet they do have their significance in showing the early development of his concerns as a writer.

Turgenev's first known attempt at verse dates from 1834, when he was a sixteen-year-old student. During the fall he produced *Steno*, a "dramatic poem" based on Byron's *Manfred*. It is no compliment to the latter to say that Turgenev's version is markedly inferior in every way. It is ostensibly written in iambic pentameter but frequently departs from this form; some words are abbreviated, others extended; occasionally syllables and words are repeated simply to assist the meter or the rhyme; and some of the monologues are a direct, and unimpressive, version of Byron's original. Nonetheless, its hero, Steno, was the first seed of what later grew into a Turgenevan "superfluous man." Intelligent, but unhappy in love, Steno loses all faith in a life, which seems to him alien and without purpose, and seeks death as an escape from his intellectual, social, and especially emotional difficulties. There is also a contrast between the intellectualizing yet cynical and despairing hero and the heroine, whose genuine love he cannot accept. The poem also bears witness to its young author's early interest in the philosophical problems of the purpose of life and the omnipresent threat of death. However, in general the poem would now be forgotten were it not Turgenev's first known work.

During the following few years Turgenev continued to experiment with verse forms. On 26 March 1837 he told his old friend Alexander Nikitenko—who incidentally thought *Steno* not completely without promise—that he was busy with a major work, *Nash vek* (*Our Age*), which would satirize the narrow-minded and prejudiced arbiters of contemporary

Russian literary taste and that, besides this, he had written about a hundred short pieces and three longer poems. Very few of these have survived; although between 1838 and the end of the 1840s Turgenev did publish a number of short poems in the literary journals *Fatherland Notes* and *Contemporary*. They are generally lyrical in mood, but most are markedly derivative and uninspired. They tend to be too "romantic" in their disillusion with life, their regret for lost or unhappy love, which is anyway fleeting, or in their unquestioning faith in the healing powers of nature. The best of them are those in a cycle of nine called collectively *Derevnya* (*The Country*), with their realistic and evocative depiction of the Russian countryside.

Turgenev's first work to attract the attention of the reading public was the "story in verse" *Parasha* of 1843. It also met with approval from the critics, led by Belinsky, who wrote that it was imbued "with a profound idea" and set in "splendid poetic verse." Although still derivative it does fall into what might be called the Russian tradition. It is clearly modeled on Pushkin's "novel in verse" *Eugene Onegin* in its description of the Russian setting, in the characterization of the hero and heroine, and in the style, if not the quality, of its composition. It also displays the influence of such narrative poems as Lermontov's *Sashka*, and indeed bore as its epigraph Lermontov's "We love, and hate, by chance." Its significance lies not so much in its rather thin story line (Parasha, a provincial girl, falls in love with a neighbor, the more experienced Viktor Alekseich, and finally marries him), nor in its theme of the decline of an idealistic young love into a not unhappy but decidedly humdrum middle age, but rather in the depiction of Parasha herself. She is unsophisticated and innocent, yet fully capable of a genuine and selfless love. Her openness and sincerity contrast sharply with the pride and disillusionment of Viktor Alekseich through whom, in the opinon of some critics, Turgenev was attempting to depict what he saw as the faults of his own generation. With his atrophied passions and his morbid preoccupation with the intellect and the ego, he has reached an impasse. Turgenev wished to define this malaise in largely social terms.[1] It could also be argued, however, that such a view relies heavily on hindsight and succumbs to the temptation to read rather too much into an author's early work. Nevertheless, with all its limitations, *Parasha* is written in more than competent verse and its story line holds together well. In short, it is "by no means a contemptible production."[2]

Of the other narrative poems, one may note *Pomeshchik* (*The Landlord*) published in 1845, and *Andrey* (1846). The latter reflects Turgenev's unhappy relationship with Tatyana, the sister of Mikhail Bakunin. The theme is one that constantly concerned Turgenev: how to end a love affair when one person (with Turgenev always the man) has ceased loving as much as the other. Here it is the woman's generous acceptance of the situation that solves the problem for the man. *The Landlord* is notable certainly for its poetic competence, but also for the unkindest of parodies of Konstantin Aksakov, the leading Slavophile of the 1840s, of which Turgenev was later deeply and deservedly ashamed. It was probably written under the strong influence of Belinsky, who admired and encouraged Turgenev's "Westernism," and displays little originality.

Finally, there is *Razgovor* (*The Conversation*) of 1845, written in the form of a dialogue between an old hermit and a young man. It may easily be seen as a description of the conflict between on the one hand the older generation of the 1820s, the Decembrists, the "seekers after truth," and their unsuccessful attempt at revolution, and on the other of the young, disillusioned idealists of the 1840s, who cannot even fail in their endeavors because they seem incapable of action of any kind. The poem ends on a markedly pessimistic note as the young man bemoans the fact that just as the old hermit's attempts at change had come to naught, so will those of his own generation. Written in fine verse, arguably the best Turgenev ever achieved, *The Conversation* also dwells on two of Turgenev's most enduring concerns about love. The first is the idea that any relationship between a man and a woman involves in varying degrees the enslavement of the man; the second is a man's heartfelt regret that he has failed to achieve happiness with a woman entirely because of his own indecision. These ideas occur repeatedly in Turgenev's more mature writings.

Early Short Stories

From the mid-1840s onward Turgenev wrote less and less poetry (and after January 1847 ceased altogether) as he turned increasingly to prose. Apart from the majority of the stories known as *A Sportsman's Sketches*, discussed in chapter 3, he published seven more short stories by 1852. The first was "Andrey Kolosov" of 1844, a love story of sorts based on characters and events from his student days; then in 1846 there were "Three Portraits," which retells a tale of the supernatural current in his mother's family, and "Breter" ("The Duellist") with its obsessive, swashbuckling hero. These were followed in 1847 by "The Jew," a slight anecdote concerning the execution of a Jewish spy during a military campaign, and "Petushkov" in the following year, the story of an unhappy love affair. In 1850 Turgenev published "The Diary of a Superfluous Man," which tells of the last days of an unsuccessful and unhappy young man. Finally in 1852 there was "Tri vstrechi" ("Three Meetings"), a semisupernatural, rather mysterious story.

Just as with his poetry, in his stories Turgenev was still up to a point experimenting with form and content, yet some of the themes he deals with here were among those to which he later returned with greater conviction. And by 1852, with the success of A Sportsman's Sketches behind him, he had clearly mastered the art of storytelling. Indeed "Three Meetings," for example, has frequently been cited as highlighting what some see as a fault of Turgenev's: so lucid, flowing, and finely wrought is his style that the reader misses the real purpose of what he is writing about. He prefers as it were to remain on the surface. This applies in particular to many of his nature descriptions, which—however evocative and superbly crafted they are in themselves—do not really add to the story. Turgenev can be carried away by his own facility at such things, and they begin to take on the suggestion of self-indulgence.[3]

For an indication of the way in which Turgenev's ideas were developing at this time, we may consider a long review article he wrote in February 1845 devoted to a Russian translation of Goethe's Faust. The piece is less of an evaluation of the translation as such than an attempt to reveal the importance of Faust for Turgenev himself and for his own generation. He sees the poem first and foremost as the "clearest and most decisive expression of romanticism," and Faust as the personification of this in that he is concerned only with himself and his own problems. On the other hand, Mephistopheles is hardly a devil on the grand scale and may seem so only to those "solitary and abstract people who are deeply confused by any little contradictions in their own lives." Goethe was, however, the first person to defend the rights of the "individual, passionate and limited man" who should be allowed "the opportunity to be happy and not to be ashamed of that happiness." (This could apply equally of course to some of Turgenev's own leading characters.) But, he continues, such a demand must be modified by current sociological ideas, for "the cornerstone for man is not man himself . . . but humanity, society." Consequently, Turgenev is concerned with the problems of individual man but in the wider context of the society he lives in, with the contrast between altruism and self-centeredness, and with the need to forsake individual rights in the service of society at large. The greatness of Faust lies precisely in the fact that Goethe does not solve this problem, and furthermore that romanticism itself cannot be expected to solve it either. There can be no reconciliation "outside the sphere of human reality" because that would be unnatural, and "we can as yet only dream of any other form of reconciliation." Turgenev admits that his conclusion might be considered "joyless," but he is concerned only with the truth. Goethe might have been a poet without equal, but people other than poets are needed now.

While his early stories do not all fit such a scheme, some of them do illustrate what he means. Although he does not attempt to reflect the individual in his society, something he would do later, Turgenev does show that his main interest is in the individual human being. Indeed, in almost everything he wrote he started not with specific ideas but with characters, and this earned him one of his more lasting reputations, as a master of portraiture. Certainly in these early stories, his skill as a portraitist overshadows the interest some of them have as love stories.

Turgenev's first published story, "Andrey Kolosov," is set in student circles, and Kolosov is introduced to the reader by the narrator in overwrought terms, as a man of special qualities whose influence over others is irresistible. Kolosov falls in love with the young Varya and soon tires of her. The narrator is asked to tell her the news, but by this time he is in love with her himself and soon finds himself engaged to be married to her. However, his affections prove shallow, and in order to extricate himself from what has become for him an embarrassing situation, he simply ceases to see her and the story ends. This is an extremely weak ending artistically, but here Turgenev is probably attempting primarily to belittle any notions of romantic and sentimental love, and so makes both Kolosov and the narrator behave in a less than admirable manner. Kolosov himself turns out in the end to be little better than a self-centered and trivial egotist, and not the paragon of virtue that Turgenev clearly originally intended. Moreover, the reader is not convinced that Kolosov is capable of loving anyone, for however short a time. The moral of the story, drawn by the narrator, is, however, significant for many of Turgenev's later works: "Gentlemen, a man who parts from a woman he has once loved at that bitter and all-important moment when he realizes against his will that his heart is no longer totally immersed in her, this man, believe me, understands the sanctity of love much better than all those petty people who from boredom or weakness continue to play on the broken strings of their weak and sentimental hearts." Yet despite this early attempt at hardheartedness, the latter type of person interested Turgenev more in the years to come, even though at the start of his career he sometimes described them with sardonic humor and even mild satire.

Other stories of the 1840s can be seen as an attempt to break away from what Turgenev saw as the contradictions of romanticism, whether that of the hero figure such as Kolosov or the more melodramatic elements found in such tales as "The Duellist," in which the central character is so outlandish and one-dimensional that it is difficult to see him other than as a purely fictional invention, and "Three Portraits," marred by a supernatural element that remains decidedly unconvincing. Turgenev does, though, appear to be seeking greater realism in character and plot. This can be sensed in "The Jew," although here it is largely unsuccessful because the characters remain stereotypes; but it is seen most clearly in "Petushkov," where Turgenev is obviously making greater efforts to depict not the unusual or special but the typical in the human condition. It is interesting also in that its uneducated and flirtatious heroine is one of the very few female characters in Turgenev who is as heartless and insincere as some of his male heroes, and yet it does contain another of its author's continuing concerns: the unhappiness and humiliation that a man's love for a woman can bring.

This theme is central also to "The Diary of a Superfluous Man." Whereas "Andrey Kolosov," "Three Portraits," and "The Jew" are constructed on the pattern of a group of people gathering together to hear one of their number relate a story, and "The Duellist" and "Petushkov" are straightforward third-person narratives, here the events are related in the form of a diary. It describes the last few days of a young man, Chulkaturin, who, dying from tuberculosis, looks back bitterly over his life and concludes that the only word to describe him is "superfluous." Chulkaturin is a failure as a human being, for none of his projects has ever succeeded thanks to weaknesses in his own personality. He shyly pays court to Lisa, the daughter of an official of standing in the local provincial community, only to be rapidly replaced in her affections by an immensely attractive prince, who, like Kolosov, once he sees that the conquest is his and that Lisa might expect too much of what to him is only an enjoyable flirtation, quickly discards her. Chulkaturin challenges the prince to a duel, fires first, and inflicts a slight flesh wound. To Chulkaturin's utter humiliation, the prince then fires into the air and considers his honor satisfied. Chulkaturin laments that he is of such little consequence as not even to be worth killing. His feelings of complete inadequacy are compounded by the fact that Lisa does not even seek consolation with him, but very soon marries a solid but unexciting neighbor. What other word is there for him, he complains, than superfluous?

The superfluous man as a type was to occupy Turgenev for some time, especially in his novels, and he viewed that type, generally speaking, as a political figure or as a victim of the Russian social system, which would parallel the views expressed in the review of *Faust*. Neither of these elements can be seen, however, in Chulkaturin's fate. His is a purely individual problem. His fatal ill-health is combined with a distressing excess of self-pity and weakness of character, and it has often been suggested that Turgenev did not give him much of a chance anyway. Still, for Turgenev even the most convincing of superfluous men were first and foremost human beings.

Plays

Most of Turgenev's early poetry and many of his short prose works were largely experimental, that is, attempts to find the most appropriate style for his writing, and within these limitations a few are reasonably successful. The same may be said of his excursions into drama, except for one of his plays, *A Month in the Country*, which is as remarkable in its genre as anything he ever wrote.

There is little doubt that Turgnev once hoped to become a major dramatist, and some contemporary critics thought he was as good a playwright as he was a short story writer. But various difficulties with the official censors, who demanded cuts and revisions and indeed banned several plays from publication or staging; indifferent performances; a tendency to underrate his own artistic achievements; and a growing interest in writing stories and then novels led him to abandon writing plays after the early 1850s even though he remained interested in the theater and dramatic technique for the rest of his life.

For nearly a generation before Turgenev wrote his first play, the Russian theater had been staging innocuous vaudevilles and romantic melodramas. Despite their poor quality they were extremely popular, especially in the provinces. A younger generation of writers and critics deplored this situation and demanded a greater realism in the theater as in other genres. Gogol's plays, especially *The Inspector General*, were considered the best examples to follow. But in the early 1840s Turgenev himself said that Gogol's plays were but the isolated achievements of a genius and unfortunately did not create a new tradition on the Russian stage. Turgenev's own first published play had a marked romantic flavor, and his second was not much more than a Russian vaudeville.

Besides *A Month in the Country*, between 1843 and 1852 Turgenev completed seven other plays: the one-act *Neostorozhnost'* (*Indiscretion*), *Bezdenezh'e* (*Lack of Money*), *Gde tonko, tam i rvetsya* (*Where It's Thin, It Tears*), *Zavtrak u predvoditelya* (*Lunch with the Master of the Nobility*), *A Provincial Lady*, the two-act *Nakhlebnik* (*A Poor Gentleman*), and a "comedy in three acts" *Kholostyak* (*The Bachelor*). There are also two short "scenes," "Razgovor na bolshoy doroge" ("Conversation on the Highway") and "Vecher v Sorrente" ("Evening in Sorrento"), together with six unfinished drafts and some outlines, plans and ideas.

The early *Indiscretion*, printed in *Fatherland Notes* in October 1843, was inspired by Mérimée's mock-Spanish *Théâtre de Clara Garul*, as indeed had been Turgenev's uncompleted *Iskushenie svyatogo Antoniya* (*Temptation of St. Anthony*). It is a tale of jealousy and murder, but there is still plenty of serenading under balconies and the like. Elements of farce are interspersed with attempts at introducing certain realistic features, notably a discussion of the subordinate position of women in a male-dominated society, although here it is the emotional rather than any social dependence that is to the fore. *Lack of Money*, written in 1845, is subtitled "Scenes from the Petersburg Life of a Young Nobleman" and bears the slight influence of Gogol in its setting and especially in its portrayal of the landowner Zhazikov and his servant Matvey, who are clearly reminiscent of Gogol's Khlestakov and Osip (*The Inspector General*). Although technically not following strictly the traditions of the vaudeville, it does retain one common device: the portrayal of a succession of characters, here the creditors who follow close upon one another into Zhazikov's apartment. But Turgenev manages to avoid caricature. He uses his skill at portraiture to present in close-up a number of carefully described types of the sort portrayed in the prose "physiological sketch" of the time, and portrays the comedy in the situation by means of contrast and contradictions between what the various characters say. It is a story about lack of money, involving not those who have never had any but those who have wasted it away, specifically by leaving their country estates (the source of their wealth) and attempting to ape the ways of the town-dwelling aristocracy. Consequently there are references here to Russia's changing social patterns, highlighted by the play's final words, spoken by Matvey: "Oh, it looks bad. Gone is the Golden Age! How the nobility has changed!" However, neither of these two plays is particularly remarkable, and both were poorly received upon publication, as was *Lack of Money* when it was first staged in 1852.

While Turgenev was living in France at the end of the 1840s he returned to writing plays. *Lunch with the Master of the Nobility*, a mild satire on the vulgarity of the landed gentry, was performed in 1849 with large cuts demanded by the censor, and frequently in the following decade. While there is little evidence elsewhere in Turgenev's writing that he could have been a good comic writer, this short play when adequately performed is extremely amusing without ever descending to the farce that one might expect in view of its incongruous and slightly absurd plot. The rather more substantial *Where It's Thin, It Tears*, written in 1848 and staged three years later for a benefit performance for an outstanding St. Petersburg actress, fails on the stage mainly because it lacks any dramatic elements. Turgenev's first attempt at putting a superfluous man on the stage, it concerns the unsuccessful attempts of Vera

Nikolaevna, the daughter of a rich widow, to induce Gorsky, the son of a neighboring landowner, to marry her. Vera's idealistic view of love and marriage is sharply contrasted with Gorsky's world-weary coldness, egotism, and sterile intellectualizing. Turgenev seems to suggest here that the ideal marriage is a unity of opposites, that, far from conflicting one with the other, apparent incompatibilities in fact complement each other, while actual, real, marriages are only a conventional ritual concealing the essential disharmony of the partners.

The two-act play *A Poor Gentleman* shows a marked maturity in Turgenev's dramatic technique, and has nothing of the romantic or vaudeville elements that detracted from his earlier plays. First written in France in 1848 at the request of the actor Mikhail Shchepkin, it was immediately banned by the theatrical censor S. A. Gedeonov, probably in retaliation for a biting review by Turgenev of one of his own plays a few years before. It was then refused publication because it portrayed the Russian gentry in a poor light, which it certainly does. Turgenev rewrote parts of it, and it was finally published in 1857 under the title *Chuzhoy khleb* (*Alien Bread*) and first performed in January 1862 in Moscow. The first act describes the return of the town-bred civil servant Eletsky with his new young wife Olga to live on her family estate. An older, impoverished nobleman, Kuzovkin (the poor gentleman of the original title), has been living there free of charge for thirty years. In the past Kuzovkin appears to have been the butt of the cruel humor and ridicule of the estate's former owner, a violent and moody man who was continually unfaithful to his wife. Kuzovkin reverts to his past role on the estate during the visit of a family friend, the base, unprincipled Tropachev. Kuzovkin is mocked, teased, and humiliated and is finally made drunk by Eletsky and Tropachev. Ostensibly in revenge, he suddenly blurts out that he is actually Olga's father. Here, at the end of the first act, most nineteenth-century productions of the play concluded, since most critics considered the second act pale and unnecessary. Actually, the second act is not only stronger dramatically than the first, its omission makes nonsense of Turgenev's intention. It shows the results of Kuzovkin's amazing declaration. He first says that his admission of paternity was an act of madness but then tells Eletsky, within the hearing of Olga, that it is indeed true. Eletsky offers Kuzovkin enough money to settle himself on his own estate in return for a retraction. Olga, who, like the audience, is never sure of the truth of the matter, convinces Kuzovkin that this would perhaps be the best solution. Kuzovkin finally accepts and leaves with an agreement that he can see his "daughter" whenever he visits the estate in the future.

Throughout his play Turgenev shows sympathy only for Kuzovkin, and to a lesser extent for Olga. He satirizes the provincial gentry at every turn for its unthinking behavior and unethical, hypocritical standards. Through a mass of psychological detail and confident stagecraft Turgenev describes the breakdown of Russia's old feudal social patterns, which is paralleled by the collapse of the psyche of the landed gentry. In all of this the real victim is neither Kuzovkin nor Eletsky, but Olga. She finds herself acting not as an individual but only as an instrument, either of her husband's self-interest or of Kuzovkin's feelings about his own identity, and ends up neither true wife nor true daughter. The picture Turgenev paints of provincial Russia is a negative one in which all positive human values are lost for mercenary or social reasons. He offers no solution to the dilemma.

If it is the woman whom Turgenev sees as victim in *A Poor Gentleman*, so it is also in *The Bachelor*, although the play is not centered on the heroine at all. *The Bachelor* is unique among Turgenev's plays in that it was written, passed by the censors (albeit with cuts involving dialogues about the sorry state of the Russian countryside, a speech in favor of women's equal rights, and all references to God, together with the alteration of one or two of the characters' names), and performed all in the same year, 1849. It relates how Moshkin, a middle-aged bachelor, has assumed the guardianship of the nineteen-year-old Masha since the death of her mother a few years earlier. For undisclosed reasons he is also taking care of an orphan, Vilitsky, who has talked Masha into marrying him. In the course of the play a friend of Vilitsky's, by playing on his snobbery, persuades him to break off the engagement, as he could find a better match elsewhere. Moshkin, horrified, proposes to her himself. At the end Moshkin is naively and excessively hopeful that they can be happy together, but Masha faces only despair and loneliness.

In many ways *The Bachelor* is similar to *A Poor Gentleman*. It used to be the tradition to seek positive elements in Turgenev's plays, and both Moshkin and Kuzovkin were interpreted as positive figures in opposition to the socially and morally decadent world around them. But this is not Turgenev's method. Rather, he uses the contrast of negatives to move the action along, and the outcome remains at best dubious. The fact that Kuzovkin and Moshkin appear better than others around them, and clearly enjoy Turgenev's sympathy to a degree, is only because they represent standards of thinking and behavior rather superior to those of the other characters. Yet by no means does this imply that they are exemplary figures. Turgenev's view of the world rarely allows such optimism.

A Month in the Country, chronologically Turgenev's seventh play, is by far the most substantial and successful of the ten he completed. It was written during the years 1848–50 while he was living in Paris. These were years when Turgenev was most swayed by the ideas of his radically minded friends Herzen and Belinsky, and when his reputation both as a writer and as a champion of the Russian peasantry was being established in Russia through the publication of various stories, especially those that made up *A Sportsman's Sketches*. The play—first called *The Student*, then *Two Women*— was sent to the editors of *Contemporary* in 1850, and they submitted it to the censors. The latter demanded major cuts, especially in some of the student Belyaev's radical speeches, and other serious changes, notably that Natalya Petrovna should be made a widow (which, of course, removed her husband Islaev from the play altogether), probably because the love of a married woman for another man was not something to be depicted on the stage. Turgenev, as was his wont, objected mildly, but nonetheless agreed to the alterations. Even so, publication was still refused. However, *A Month in the Country*, as it was then called, was passed for publication in 1855 with all the demands of the censors satisfied. It next appeared in 1869 in an edition of Turgenev's works with some minor changes introduced by Turgenev and with Islaev's part restored.

Much has been made of Turgenev's debt here to Balzac's *La Marâtre* (*The Stepdaughter*), which had been staged with a modicum of success in 1848 in Paris, where Turgenev might well have seen it. There are clearly some plot similarities. Both comedies (although it is odd that Turgenev should have used this description) concern the love of a young married woman (Gertrude/Natalya Petrovna) and her much younger stepdaughter/ward (Pauline/Vera) for a young man the former employs (Ferdinand/Belyaev). The older woman tries to remove her rival by arranging for her to marry a quite unsuitable older bachelor (Godard/Bolshintsov). There are also similarities in the roles of a cynical, yet dispassionate and observing, doctor (Vernon/Shpigelsky) and a young son (Napoléon/Kolya). However, the atmosphere and the entire dramatic conflict are different, if only because Turgenev gives a central role to Rakitin, the man unhappily in love, with all the bitterness and regret this involves, and because he sets his play in the milieu he knew best—that of the Russian country house inhabited by representatives of the minor gentry. Gone too are Balzac's romantic techniques and melodramatic tendencies. Moreover, *La Marâtre* now rests in deserved obscurity, while *A Month in the Country* is still successfully and regularly produced, and that should lead the modern reader or playgoer to disregard whatever debt Turgenev might owe to Balzac.

A Month in the Country was first staged in Moscow in 1872, with cuts with which Turgenev, characteristically, readily concurred. Some twenty years before he had written that it was not really a play anyway but a novel in dramatic form unsuitable for the stage. When it proved to be no great success with either the public or the critics Turgenev was only confirmed in his mistaken view. In 1879 the young actress Marya Savina chose it for her benefit performance, asked Turgenev to cut it a little—but only on grounds of length, for a complete performance would take close to five hours—and played the part of Vera. It was a remarkable success, and Savina's performance ensured that the play gradually entered the regular repertory. A production of 1909 at the Moscow Art Theatre with Stanislavsky directing and playing the part of Rakitin and Chekhov's widow Olga Knipper as Natalya Petrovna made it famous and established the interpretation it is usually given today, at least outside its native country. Although Stanislavsky's friend and collaborator Vladimir Nemirovich-Danchenko first thought the play was a faithful reflection of a former, unchanging Russia with all the social criticism that implied, even though it was the Russia in which Turgenev had been brought up, Stanislavsky saw it as a psychological study and played down its social or political aspects. Indeed, the action of the play is almost entirely psychological, and this makes it particularly demanding to act and especially rewarding to watch. Although basically this aspect of the play has led many later commentators to see it as only a precursor of Chekhov's work, in it Turgenev combines his skill at portraiture with his ability to sketch the changing and often conflicting emotions that afflict men and women in love. With the finest sensibility to language and through immensely skillfully written dialogue—often it is what is not said, although clearly understood, that is of importance—Turgenev depicts the barely or not immediately noticeable changes that take place in relationships, the elation and the doubts, the jealousies, justified or not, the hopes and fears, the rises and falls in emotional intensity, and the changing patterns of love and hate among the characters. Crucial to the psychological interpretation of the play is the role of Natalya Petrovna and her relations to and effects upon the characters whose misfortune it is to come under her sway. Stanislavsky saw her as a hothouse plant that really wished it could grow in the fresh air and open fields. Perhaps Turgenev reflects this in that he sets only one of the five acts out of doors. If the "indoors" side of Natalya's personality is expressed in her marriage to Islaev, then her dreams center on the young student Belyaev. Her moods are constantly changing, and she infuriates and confuses those around her. Extremely emotional and selfish, she frequently acts without the slightest regard for the feelings of others. She discounts her husband, bullies and terrorizes Vera out of her spontaneous love for the dithering Belyaev and into marriage with Bolshintsov, falls in love with Belyaev, who cannot cope with either the apparent intensity or the only too obvious fluctuations in her feelings and behavior, but yet refuses to go away with him. She remains faithful to her husband, whom she probably respects but certainly does not love. In the process she loses her faithful admirer Rakitin, through whom Turgenev expressed much of his own view of himself.

Overall *A Month in the Country* is pessimistic about the human condition. Happiness is a possibility, but is never attained. Belyaev is almost alone in believing that love is a positive thing that can lead to happiness, but Rakitin, in the most bitter passage in the whole play, does his best to disillusion him. Love, whether in itself ostensibly happy or unhappy, can lead only to misery in the end. In the whole of Turgenev's writings there is only one love relationship that runs smoothly, that between Elena and Insarov in *On the Eve*, but even that ends with the death of Insarov. As will become apparent from some of his later works, in Turgenev there is an almost intimate connection between love and death. The happiness he permits his characters is always overshadowed by the sometimes unadmitted but nonetheless ever-present knowledge that death, either literal or emotional, waits to take its due.

Although the psychological interpretation of *A Month in the Country* would seem today the most satisfactory, Turgenev also offered some social and political comment. The fact that contemporary censors deleted material they considered unsuitable is ample evidence that Turgenev originally intended to portray rather more than an interplay of emotions. Couched in lyrical terms and set among the nostalgic charms of a Russian gentry class in decline, the play contrasts two social groupings: on the one hand the old, out-of-date, aimless gentry class of Natalya Petrovna, Rakitin, and Bolshintsov, living out their days in the idle pursuit of happy love but doomed to ultimate frustration, and on the other the younger, ambitious, idealistic, hopeful, and hardworking section of the community, that of Vera, Belyaev, and the servants, whose day is about to dawn. The highly observant but disillusioned Dr. Shpigelsky, both in his personal history and in his actual words and behavior throughout the play, expresses explicitly much overt criticism of the old order with almost vicious delight. He sees the stupidity of the landowners and the decline of the rural economy; he attacks the officer class and describes the appalling conditions that prevailed in his childhood and have not improved since. Such matters would not have been lost on the contemporary audience, and thus the play contains a social and political element that should not be completely ignored. But to stress it at the expense of a fascinating if gently pessimistic examination of the lives and loves of its characters is to miss the play's most enduring component.[4]

Chapter Three
A Reputation Established

A Sportsman's Sketches

A *Sportsman's Sketches*, a collection of stories largely describing the life and customs of the Russian peasants and their masters, was written for the most part while Turgenev was living in France and Germany at the end of the 1840s and beginning of the 1850s. It established his reputation as the leading Russian writer of the day and caused him to be exiled to Spasskoe for a period of some eighteen months. The collection consists of twenty-five stories, varying in length from just over 3,000 words to 12,000 words, although the majority of them run to about 8,000 words. All but four were printed in *Contemporary* between 1847 and 1851, and these twenty-one, together with "Two Landowners," comprised the first edition published as a book in 1852. Of the remaining three, "The End of Chertopkhanov," by far the longest, first appeared in *Messenger of Europe* in 1872, "The Living Relic" in *Skladchina* (*Pooling*), a miscellany published in 1874 to aid victims of a terrible famine in Samara, and, finally, "The Knocking" was included in the first volume of the 1874 edition of Turgenev's collected works.

This series, which established Turgenev as a prominent writer, was started almost by chance. Turgenev's friends, Nekrasov and Panaev, who had just bought *Contemporary*, wrote to him inquiring whether he might have any contributions for their journal. Although at the time he was toying with the idea of giving up writing (something he did periodically), he did send, rather halfheartedly, a number of poems and reviews and a short story entitled "Khor and Kalinych." When this was printed Panaev added the subtitle "From a Sportsman's Sketches." However, the second story, "Petr Petrovich Karataev," appeared without the subtitle, and it was not until the publication of the third, "Ermolay and the Miller's Wife," that it became clear that Turgenev had decided to continue writing similar stories under the general title *A Sportsman's Sketches*. It is possible that the idea for such a collection was derived from *Souvenirs de chasses*, a short book published by Pauline Viardot's husband Louis in 1846. Turgenev was also well acquainted with George Sand's stories of rural life in France and Marie Edgeworth's novels set in the Irish countryside, and these might also have provided suitable models for him. And many earlier Russian writers had dealt with the peasants and their masters—Radishchev, Krylov, Pushkin, and Gogol, for example. The greatest influence, however, on their content, if not their style, was probably Belinsky. More than anyone else it was he who had called upon Russian writers to discuss social and political issues so far as possible under the prevailing conditions of censorship and thereby point up the manifold shortcomings of contemporary Russian life. However much Belinsky admired individuals for their intellect, and consequently made serious demands upon the Russian intelligentsia, he nonetheless considered all men created equal. He stressed the clear injustices suffered by the impoverished town-dwellers of his day, but attacked most of all the whole unjust institution of serfdom. Turgenev himself was no stranger to the iniquities such a system encouraged. As a young man he had been revolted by his mother's mistreatment of her serfs. When he had tried to remonstrate with her, she had said she did not really know what he was complaining about as all her serfs were well fed and housed and, what was more, were paid a wage. All was well with them. Turgenev had noticed, however, that most of them lived in constant fear of her. His mother had agreed, but claimed that that was exactly as it should be, as was her absolute power over them. She saw nothing at all reprehensible in her behavior, quite the reverse, in fact. People should know their place.

Yet whatever influences there may have been, the stories themselves all ultimately stem from Turgenev's own personal experience. Himself a member of the landowning gentry class, possessor of estates and peasants, an avid shooter and lover of the countryside, Turgenev was writing about what he knew best. Many of the events he describes actually happened, and some of the characters, both peasants and landowners, are based on people Turgenev knew. Perhaps the fact that most of the stories were written while Turgenev was living abroad explains the vividness of the portraits he paints, even their gentle nostalgia, albeit a nostalgia for the very recent past, and a sense that certainly things must be changed but a regret that they cannot be just improved.

Thus Turgenev's own personal experiences, added to Belinsky's demands on a writer on the one hand and his friendship with Turgenev and his sincere admiration for some of his earlier writings on the other, set the tone for the *Sketches*. Their form was determined by the contemporary popularity of the so-called physiological sketch, where the main purpose was not to treat characters as specific and interesting individuals but rather as types, and in so doing to depict the most representative elements in society. It was only natural that "sketches" on similar themes should be gathered together into a book to give the reader a more complete picture of society.

The first story in *A Sportsman's Sketches* certainly satisfies the contemporary demands. "Khor and Kalinych" begins with a definite and intentional contrast between one type of peasant and another, very different, but, according to Turgenev, equally characteristic. From the outset of the series he attempts to break down one of the more enduring illusions of his own social (and peasant-owning) class: the notion that the peasantry is homogeneous. He seeks to humanize the peasant, to give him some individual existence, and to make his readers, most of whom would be owners of serfs too, realize this fact and then conclude that the situation was not ideal and consequently at least to think about changing things for the better. Although the two peasants, Khor and Kalinych, might be a little too well differentiated and a bit idealized, the sociological intentions behind the story and the manner in which it is written are very clear. While such intentions are detectible in the majority of the stories, it cannot be claimed that they each follow a strict pattern, and the order of presentation that Turgenev finally chose for them in 1874 does not coincide with the chronology of their composition or original publication. The fact that he was still adding to the collection more than twenty years after most of its stories had first appeared might suggest that he never considered the series complete, or even perhaps that he was never satisfied with it. Indeed, he published other stories, quite different in intention and content, while the majority of the *Sketches* were appearing. While it is true that Turgenev was rarely satisfied with anything he wrote, perhaps without the initial success of "Khor and Kalinych" (and a precarious financial situation caused by his mother's failure to provide him with an allowance) he might not have persevered—and Russian literature would never have had one of its undoubted masterpieces.

Although the stories cannot be seen as all of a piece, most of them do have certain characteristics exemplified by "Khor and Kalinych." First of all, the reader is introduced to the narrator, who has left his home to go shooting game. Turgenev uses this device frequently to get the narrative in motion. Yet we learn very little about the narrator himself; and, indeed, Turgenev goes to great lengths to make him as unobtrusive as possible. Although the narrator often falls into conversation with the characters he wishes to describe or whose lives he wants to relate, on occasion Turgenev has him resort to the less than admirable tactic of eavesdropping, hiding himself the better to observe or listen, or pretending to be asleep. His role throughout is to observe and report what he sees, not to instigate the action or even to comment on it especially. He is clearly an intelligent, observant, inquisitive man who enjoys noting his experiences. But whatever the rights, or rather wrongs, of the pictures he draws of the lives of the peasantry and the landowners, a life of which he is himself an integral part, he does not suggest any path to improvement. Only very rarely does he explicitly suggest that anything is seriously wrong. For example, in "Two Landowners" he points to the horrible, cramped huts in which the peasants are forced to live: there is not a tree to be seen, and no pond, just a single well that is of no use; moreover, the landowner has even taken the peasants' old hempfields from them. The landowner argues that the land redistribution forced upon him will bring no good to anyone, and that as for ponds and hempfields he really has not the slightest idea about such things: "I am just a simple man and I have old-fashioned ways. In my way of thinking, if you're the master, you're the master, and if you're a peasant, you're a peasant. And that's that." It might have been Turgenev's mother speaking. The narrator does not pursue the matter: "It goes without saying that such a lucid and convincing argument was unanswerable." This is of course tongue-in-cheek, but the lack of any commitment on the narrator's part to push for change stems not necessarily from indifference or any feeling of superiority toward the peasants but largely from ignorance, an ignorance shared equally by peasant and master. The narrator's urge to describe what he sees might be motivated by a wish to dispel some of this ignorance, an ignorance that Turgenev clearly felt was shared by most of the landowning class. But the narrator has no effect at all on the world he describes. "Kasyan of the Beautiful Lands" contains a remarkable passage where the narrator stops to rest in a forest clearing, lies down on his back, and gazes upward to admire the peaceful play of the tangled leaves against the far-off, radiant sky. He cannot express in words how joyful, gentle, and delectable is the mood that enters his heart as he is absorbed into the bosom of nature itself. This feeling can be seen as a metaphor for his lack of initiative in the world he inhabits. If he becomes part of an unchanging nature, then no action is either necessary or indeed possible and consequently any responsibility he might feel for the life he leads is removed.

In some ways this irresponsibility is paralleled by the behavior of other landowners and members of the nobility Turgenev depicts. In "Raspberry Water," for example, a peasant walks miles from an estate to see his master in Moscow (one of many examples of landowners who have deserted their estates) to ask him to lower his rent, or to move him somewhere cheaper, or to let him work for his dues rather than pay them in cash. The master "simply threw me out. He said, 'How dare you come straight to me. That's what the estate manager's for. You ought to report to him . . . and where can I move you to anyway? You pay your arrears first!' He got very angry." The peasant's meek acceptance of the situation obviates any need for responsibility on the part of the master. In "Hamlet of Shchigrovsky District" the men gathering for a provincial dinner party are either just putting on airs or afraid that their dissembling will be recognized for what it is. The emptiness of their words reflects the political vacuum in which they live out their pointless lives. In "Ovsyanikov the Freeholder" Turgenev points to a possible cause for this. The smaller landowners spend all their time working for the government and thus neglect their estates or keep moving from one place to another, and "as for the bigger sort, well, there's no recognizing them." Ovsyanikov might idealize the nobility in history (and there are convincing arguments that since its historical "golden age" during the reign of Catherine the Great in the second half of the eighteenth century the nobility had been gradually, and indeed helplessly, declining), but he is correct about their present condition. The easy access to government service with its attractions for those interested only in maintaining the status quo and the feeble continuity of land ownership both lead to a lack of interest in the land and thus the peasantry, and also to the economic decline of the countryside. So both landowner and peasant are caught in the same trap. Consequently, the narrator's lack of action reflects the fact that no one could take effective action in the social and political context of that day.

Although the existence of a strict literary censorship prevented any direct attack on the institution of serfdom—and this was not usually Turgenev's method anyway—there is no doubt that a very grim picture emerges from these stories. However different, for example, the personalities of Khor and Kalinych are (differences that Turgenev later enlarged upon in his essay *Hamlet and Don Quixote*), the lives of Khor and Kalinych are not enviable in any way. Both of them are far from unintelligent and they are both individuals, although they do each possess certain characteristics that make them typical of the class of peasant and type of personality Turgenev wishes to describe. Furthermore, Turgenev portrays them as sympathetically as the demands of accuracy will allow. But the same cannot be said about the landowner Polutykin. Although there is no obvious criticism of him, he is presented in a mildly ridiculous light with his stammer, his unsuccessful but ever-hopeful courting of all the marriageable young ladies of the district, his frequent repetition of an anecdote that only he finds amusing, and his devotion to what he considers a form of French cuisine, "the secret of which . . . consisted in completely altering the natural taste of each and every dish." If in "Khor and Kalinych" Turgenev does not portray the peasant in the most positive light, he depicts the landowner with at best a certain irony. Furthermore, the contemporary reader would notice Turgenev's concentration not on the landowner but on the peasants.

The third story of the series, "Ermolay and the Miller's Wife," is more clearly critical of the ills of serfdom. While out shooting with one of his constant peasant companions the narrator spends a night at the miller's house and overhears a conversation in which Ermolay asks the miller's wife, Arina, who is ill and desperately unhappy, to leave her husband for him. She refuses. In a later conversation, this time between the narrator and Arina, the full story is revealed. Bought by a landowner and employed as maid to his wife, Arina becomes fond of a peasant on the estate and becomes pregnant. So outraged is the landowner at her "ingratitude" to him that he has her head publicly shaved and then dismisses her, sending the father of the child to the army. Later the miller buys her freedom and marries her. The lightness of Turgenev's touch and the wondrous descriptions of the natural surroundings, especially a remarkable one of sunset in the forest, tend to reduce the impact of the events related, but nonetheless the inhumanity of a system that allows such arbitrary treatment of human beings is abundantly clear.

Turgenev's magnificent—though nearly always understated—descriptive power is equally apparent in, for example, "Kasyan of the Beautiful Lands," based on what Turgenev had learned locally about the life and trials of certain religious sectarians. Kasyan himself is a remarkable portrait. Apparently a member of some mysterious religious sect, Kasyan not only denounces blood sports—which take place not to provide food, that might be their only justification, but "just for fun"—but also expresses the desire to escape the harsh realities of the established way of life and enter the fantasy world of peasant folklore, where leaves do not fall from the trees in autumn, where golden apples grow on silver boughs, and everyone lives in peace, harmony, and happiness. The plea for some sort of justice for the peasantry is, however, still muted and implicit, however sympathetically Turgenev portrays the dissenters.

"Two Landowners" is far more explicit in its depiction of the widespread hardhearted and selfish brutality of the landowners. Using a technique like that employed in "Khor and Kalinych," Turgenev contrasts two landowners: a retired general, Khvalinsky, who has never seen active service and knows nothing of military matters, and whose attitude toward his estate is comparable. However, if his inactivity and incompetence in the army were probably beneficial to the troops under his command those same traits have quite the opposite effect on his serfs. Nevertheless, since he gets a satisfactory living from his estate he considers himself a model landowner, and is thought of as such in the district. Nor is his the greatest of intellects. When it was pointed out to him that his store-barns frequently caught fire and so much of his grain was being lost, he ordered that no corn be placed in the barns until all the fires had been extinguished. The second landowner, Stegunov, is completely different except that, like Khvalinsky, he is a bachelor. A landowner in the old style, he possesses five hundred serfs and takes only a superficial interest in his estates. For example, fearing to be thought behind the times he purchases a threshing machine but leaves it in a barn for ten years, thinking his duty done. His house is old, as is all the furniture in it; everything is old-fashioned and uncared for despite his many servants, but he lives happily and well, entrusting the management of his estates to an aging peasant-bailiff and that of his house to a wrinkled, tight-fisted old woman. Everything is as it should be. Such gently mocking portraits belie the awful results of his style of living: impoverished peasants who fear their master's arbitrary outbursts of violence, as well as his cruelty and prejudices. This attitude is reflected in Stegunov's treatment of a young village priest, who displays the unforgivable faults of preaching sermons and not drinking: "Unheard of for a priest!" The real tragedy of the situation is that those who suffer most from Stegunov's behavior and attitudes—his peasants—are so cowed by the system that they even consider it normal and proper. The butler who is flogged for no good reason can only say that it served him right: "You don't get beaten for nothing here. . . . That's not how things are arranged here. . . . Our master's not like that. . . . You won't find another master like ours anywhere else in the province." And the narrator responds: "Well, that's old-style Russia for you." Like the peasants, he can do nothing. The irony is, though, that "old-style Russia" has not really changed.

The peasant conviction that the landowner has complete control over their lives is seen most clearly in "The Bailiff," where Turgenev acknowledged his debt to Belinsky and expressed his support for the latter's deeply felt plea for justice in Russia's social life and institutions voiced in his famous "Letter to Gogol," written in unbelieving response to Gogol's eccentric *Selected Passages from Correspondence with Friends* with its poorly thought-out and obscure Slavophile doctrines. Of all the stories in *A Sportsman's Sketches* "The Bailiff" is by far the most outspoken attack on the exploitation of the peasantry. Turgenev is at his most cutting in his portrayal of the dandy and petty tyrant Penochkin, whose cruel treatment of his peasants is tempered only by a wish to appear progressive to others but which is made more striking by the calm and polite manner in which it is meted out. Equally perceptive is Turgenev's presentation of the drunken, fawning bailiff, Sofron, whose opinion of the peasants under his control is only a reflection of Penochkin's. Indeed, the worse he treats them, the more he thinks he is carrying out Penochkin's wishes.

Not all Turgenev's peasant overseers are like Sofron, but the effect is similar. "The Lone Wolf" describes an extremely conscientious and hard-working peasant forester. He is dedicated to his master; he is honest, even virtuous. The hatred and fear his fellow peasants feel toward him never make him consider altering his strict moral code. His sense of duty and honor, which he views as part and parcel of his job, also causes much hardship, and even death, to those under his control, as he keeps his master in inexcusable luxury. If the poverty of the peasants forces them to steal in order to survive, he would not overlook the matter, for then he would be blamed himself, and "there is no need to pamper the likes of them." Although his character is nobler and his motives in the circumstances more understandable, and though he does show, despite himself, one flash of fellow feeling, the effect of most of his actions is as dire as those of Sofron. In their different ways they are both also victims of a depersonalizing system. And yet once more Turgenev suggests that neither peasant nor master is capable of changing anything.

Quite obviously stories such as these were seen at the time as a plea for the better treatment of the peasantry. They had a real influence on the mood that led—after the end of the Crimean War and the advent of a new czar, Alexander II—to the changes culminating in the emancipation of the peasants in 1861. But not all of them are so clearly condemnatory of the situation that prevailed then.

Indeed, some of the stories, particularly those that concentrate not on the peasants but specifically on their masters ("Petr Petrovich Karataev," "My Neighbor Radilov," "The District Apothecary"), deal hardly at all with the problems of serfdom, even though they are placed in the same geographical and social environment. They have a more strict story line and are best read as unhappy love stories, movingly told and without a trace of the sentimentality to which their content might all too easily have led. This applies also to "The Rendezvous," the only story in the *Sketches* that describes a genuine love relationship among the peasants. Perhaps Turgenev felt he would be on surer ground to limit himself to describing peasant life and customs instead of attempting a love story and running the risk of presenting the emotions and sensibilities of his own class rather than that part of the peasant personality of which he was ignorant. Belinsky had commented that Turgenev was incapable of drawing characters whose like he had not met in real life and whose behavior and motivation he did not understand, and Turgenev himself later admitted that he wrote exclusively for his own class and drew from it the subject matter of most of his best writings.

Several further stories concentrate on matters other than serfdom. While, for example, "Tatyana Borisovna and Her Nephew" shows the landowners in a poor light, it is primarily an attack on the pretensions of amateurs of art, personified in the nephew who, besides being a sponger on all those susceptible to him, has no talent at all. "Bezhin Meadow," among the most memorable tales of the whole collection, is an early attempt at a tale of the supernatural. It has very little social message at all even though the restricting presence of serfdom can be sensed. The opening description of a beautiful and hot July day shows Turgenev at his brilliant best. The feeling of mystery and suspense he builds up as the narrator returns from a shooting trip as night falls, and loses his way, is no less effective in establishing a mood and arousing the interest, and foreboding, of the reader. The narrator falls in with five peasant boys, whose differing personalities he sketches lightly but tellingly, and relates their conversation around the camp fire. They talk of ghosts, water fairies, eclipses, and superstitions. A feeling of considerable unease is skillfully established, and the presence of death is almost tangible. But all finally fall asleep until morning. Turgenev's description of the early morning as the narrator leaves for home rivals the opening passage in its splendid evocation of summer days. Both of them reflect the joyful innocence of childhood remembered with a touch of regretful nostalgia.

As might be expected from some of his earlier short stories, Turgenev's preoccupation with "superfluity" appears, in only slightly disguised form, in some *Sketches*, for example, in "Death" and most notably in "Hamlet of Shchigrovsky District." The former is artistically the least unified of all the stories in the collection, being a series of reflections on the theme of death, but its effect is no less for that. It begins with a contrast, a device frequently used in the *Sketches*, between the beauty of nature and its cruelty, factors the narrator notes with joy for the one and regret for the other. Both aspects of nature, though, are treated with equal indifference by the peasants. A contractor is fatally injured by a falling tree; just before he dies he begs forgiveness for any injury he may have caused his fellow peasants and then tries to organize his personal affairs. "What an astonishing thing is the death of a Russian peasant," reflects the narrator. "His state of mind just before death could be called neither one of indifference nor one of stupidity; he dies as if he is performing a ritual act, coldly and simply." He then recalls the deaths of two other peasants. One awaited his end calmly while those around him silently carried on with their work, not out of any lack of feeling or a need to do something to take their minds off what was happening, but simply because there was nothing else to do. The other, who had internal injuries following an accident, wished against all advice to return home because "if I don't, God knows what mess they'll get themselves into." The narrator recalls these deaths in a sympathetic but matter-of-fact manner. He reserves his compassion for Avenir Sorokoumov, a meek and mild "eternal student" who earns a meager living as tutor to a landowner's children. He is kind, rather timid, sensitive yet enthusiastic. But he is dying from tuberculosis, and his gentle nature is as useless to him when he faces death as it has been in life. A sense of the ephemeral nature of everything valuable in the human being was strong within Turgenev and yet saddened him at the same time. He sees it as made worthwhile only by the beauty it is capable of inspiring, an idea dealt with at greater length in "The Singers" where a singing contest is won by the peasant most able to touch the listeners' hearts. Although Turgenev avoided sentimentalism by describing a drunken celebration at the end that nicely counterbalances the previous events, the story reflects more than any other the almost heartrending sadness of rural existence.

"Hamlet of Shchigrovsky District" deals hardly at all with the problems of serfdom, being more concerned with what Turgenev saw as the main reason for the ineffectiveness of his own generation (and perhaps his own too)—its Hamletism. It begins with one of Turgenev's very rare richly humorous passages where he unobtrusively but mockingly dissects provincial society in describing the arrival of a local dignitary and a dinner he is attending. The bulk of the story concerns the life of an anonymous "Vasily Vasilych" told to the narrator late on the night of the dinner when neither can sleep. That life includes a series of misfortunes, of unhappy loves and marriage, of attempting much and failing everything, of trying to make a name for himself in a world he gradually but increasingly comes to despise, a lack of concern for his estates, a failure in the end to reconcile himself to his own faults of character except in self-disgust, and an unhealthy concentration on his own thoughts and behavior, none of which contain an ounce of the originality he so craves but which he knows he does not possess. Thus does Turgenev describe the idealism, the loss of illusion, and the subsequent inability to act purposefully that he believed characterized his own generation. It is symbolic of this failure, the refusal to accept responsibility for one's actions or words, that when the narrator awakes in the morning the "Hamlet" has already left. Although satire is confined to the opening, the concentration on the "Hamlet's" unfortunate life and personality remains gently comic. And yet, considering that this is but one of the *Sketches*, the reader is left with the uncomfortable impression that if men such as he, an educated and privileged member of the landowning gentry, could not succeed, what hope can there be for anyone else? As Lermontov had suggested a decade or so previously in *A Hero of Our Time*, he can diagnose the disease but has no idea at all of any cure. Perhaps this is the

essence of Turgenev's writing. It is not without significance that whatever social, political, or even philosophical, intent may have informed the *Sketches*,
Turgenev ends the series with "Forest and Steppe," a short chapter describing
the beauties of the Russian countryside. Did Turgenev absolve himself from
all responsibility for the iniquities he described in the series, just as his narrator seems to have done? He reminds his readers that the main purpose of the
Sketches, and that which makes life itself worth living, is the joy of shooting
expeditions, especially in the forest regions of Russia. Yet the reader cannot
help realizing that there are far more important problems to be faced, however much he might regret their interference with the enjoyment of what life
has to offer.

When viewed from this perspective, when the conditions of life Turgenev
describes have changed (although, *mutatis mutandis*, readers of, say,
Solzhenitsyn's "Matryona's Home" might disagree), when the social and political environment has changed so markedly, *A Sportsman's Sketches* can be
judged on criteria other than those applied by his contemporaries. On the one
hand it may be considered a stage—a definitely important stage—in
Turgenev's development as a writer, as the first significant proof of his maturity, and as evidence of his growing control over his subject matter, an increasing competence in the techniques of writing, and a foretaste of themes
and ideas to come. On the other hand, and more important, the *Sketches* is
one of the most beautifully written books in any language, a lyrical, nostalgic, gently humorous, marvelously evocative, vivid description of the Russian countryside and its inhabitants. It is Turgenev's honesty in presenting
what he sees, his artistic sensibility, his precise, deceptively simple, but exquisite prose with its carefully chosen vocabulary, his almost unfailing skill in se-
lecting just the right word or expression, the lack of any conscious literary
devices or seeking effect: qualities such as these have helped the *Sketches* survive the passage of time and make it still a positive joy to read. Turgenev
achieved greater things with his novels, yet to come, but even if he had ceased
writing after the publication of the first edition of the *Sketches* in 1852, he
would have bequeathed later generations a work of lasting value. *A
Sportsman's Sketches* is Turgenev's least questionable literary achievement.
Modest as ever about his abilities as a writer, he wrote to his friend Annenkov
in 1852: "I am glad . . . it has come out. I think it will remain the little I have
cast into the treasure chest of Russian literature. . . . Much of it is just not
what it should be—too much salt or underdone, but there are other notes
that are pitched exactly right and not out of tune, and it is these that will save
the whole book." He need not have been nearly so diffident.

Stories and Novellas

Although during most of the 1850s Turgenev turned his attention primarily to novels combining a love story with comment on contemporary Russian society, he continued to publish stories. In many of these he repeated and developed earlier themes and preoccupations, but he also introduced new ones, and all in all his reputation as Russia's leading writer of the period was enhanced, although in the 1860s his popularity was overtaken by that of Tolstoy and Dostoyevski. In this period Turgenev searched for a new style of writing, as both "A Quiet Spot" and "Two Friends" show. The title of the former is ironic: a country backwater is the setting for a passionate conflict that ends in death. A young, somewhat prim, landowner, Vladimir Sergeevich, visits a neglected estate of his and calls on a widowed neighbor while there. His sister-in-law Marya is involved in an intense love affair with the story's hero Veretev, a charming young man whose interests, however, do not extend much beyond wine and women. His unfeeling desertion of Marya leads ultimately to her suicide. While his careless behavior, shallow emotions, and irresponsibility mark him as a typical man of the 1840s, Turgenev's sympathies are clearly with him rather than with the staid, conventional, reliable, but uninspired Vladimir Sergeevich. There is also a hint that the impressionable Marya is strongly affected by a reading of Pushkin's poem "The Upas-Tree," a point more fully examined in "Faust."

In "Two Friends" Turgenev uses the device of contrast so successfully employed in "Khor and Kalinych" to reflect the thoughts and behavior of the Russian minor gentry of the time. Krupitsyn is a traditional Russian landowner as envisaged by Turgenev, while Vyazovnin has a veneer of Western European culture. Against Krupitsyn's advice Vyazovnin marries an unsophisticated, gentle young girl. Not unexpectedly, he soon tires of her and departs for the fleshpots of Paris, where he is killed in a duel. Later Krupitsyn marries his widow and the two spend the rest of their lives uneventfully but happily. Although Turgenev would show himself at his most Russophile in *Home of the Gentry*, which appeared a few years later, "Two Friends" hints strongly that his sympathies, certainly at this time, lay more with the virtues of the traditional Russian way of life rather than with the superficial attractive but ultimately futile Western European (or at least Parisian) values.

Turgenev was a regular and accomplished, if not always prompt, correspondent. While abroad he looked upon his letters as a means of "talking to his friends," as a way of keeping in touch with what was happening in the Russia he loved and missed. He often used letters in his fiction as a literary device, but "A Correspondence" and "Faust" are specifically epistolary in construction.

In the summer of 1854 Turgenev became fond of a distant cousin named Olga Turgeneva. Many of his friends thought he would marry her, and there is little doubt that he seriously contemplated the idea. Their relationship, however, did not develop, and Turgenev incorporated some of its aspects in "A Correspondence." First begun in 1844 and then laid aside, it was completed at the very end of 1854. It is cast as an exchange of fifteen letters between the mortally ill Aleksey Petrovich, who is living in Dresden, and a friend from his past, Marya Aleksandrovna. Their correspondence lasts from March 1840 to September 1842.

In one sense "A Correspondence" is a further attempt by Turgenev to analyze the "superfluous man" of the 1840s. Aleksey looks back over his short life and concludes that it has been wasted. This strikes him as typical of all Russians like him: it is simply their destiny never to achieve anything. He reminds Marya of the time they both were young (for Turgenev anyone beyond the age of thirty is no longer young). They were pure, idealistic, hopeful, full of ideas, and believed in a better future. Yet nothing came of this because they only thought they were all of those things, they only thought they loved each other, and their thoughts never led to action. Because they were the people they were, they should never have expected to succeed. Here as so often, Turgenev describes a problem for which he has no solutions.

More important, however, "A Correspondence" illustrates other themes that would be constants in Turgenev's writings over the years. Aleksey initiates his correspondence with Marya in an attempt to overcome his loneliness and perhaps to revive their former affection for each other. Marya is unhappy and unmarried, and although at first reluctant she does agree to correspond. Their previous mutual love is indeed rekindled. At one point, however, she accuses him of excessive introspection. Has he ever thought, she asks, what it is like to be a Russian *woman*? She dreams of love, of *him*. He appears. She is deliriously happy. Then he grows tired of her and leaves, and it is so easy for him. She becomes sad and lonely. She would have idolized him, but there are no heroes in Russia anymore. What can she do except seek happiness in her home? Later Marya receives a proposal from a neighbor, a young, well-educated, good, and honest landowner who clearly loves her. But she also finds him limited and spiritless. What should she do? Aleksey advises her against marriage. Women, he writes, are always superior to men anyway; she must not feel ashamed of becoming an old maid. "It's not happiness but human dignity that is the chief aim in life," he asserts. This is easy for him to say, and his advice is not purely altruistic, but in letter 12 Aleksey decides that since they are both unhappy he must do something to remedy the situation. He plans to return to Russia and see her again. In her reply Marya looks forward to their reunion with a mixture of joy and fear. However, six months later, after writing him many times, she hears nothing more. It is a further eighteen months before he replies. He had not returned as he promised because he had fallen passionately in love with a ballet dancer, who was not at all intelligent but extremely beautiful. After a year she had simply cast him off. How could he have behaved like that, he asks. "In actual life it turns out that real love is a feeling utterly unlike what we imagined. Indeed, love is not a feeling at all, but an illness. . . . In love there is no equality. . . . one person is a slave, the other the master. . . . Love is a fetter and the heaviest to bear." Aleksey does not apologize for his behavior and urges Marya to resign herself to life's unhappiness, as he has done now that he faces death. Such ideas were to become increasingly common with Turgenev.

"Faust" was written in a few days during the summer of 1856. It consists of nine letters, all from Pavel Aleksandrovich B. to a friend, Semen Nikolaevich V., and so is a first-person narrative cast in letter form. Like "A Correspondence," it contains several themes typical of Turgenev. There is the evil influence of imaginative literature upon those unprepared for it (as in "A Quiet Spot"); there is the effect of the supernatural upon human affairs, and the suggestion of the impossibility of a happy love between a man and a woman lasting more than a short time; and finally there is the apparently inevitable connection between love and death. "Faust" relates how, some years after their first friendship, the hero meets Vera Nikolaevna, who is now married. Brought up extremely strictly, Vera had been forbidden by her mother, among other things, to read literature, and especially poetry. Pavel, who had never understood such a prohibition, begins to visit her at home and then to read her the first part of Goethe's *Faust*. This stimulates her feelings for Pavel to the point where she avows her love for him. However, on the way to a rendezvous with him she is stopped by an apparition of her dead mother, falls ill with a mysterious fever, and dies soon afterward. Pavel's final words undoubtedly express Turgenev's own feelings: "In conclusion I will say this; I have derived one conviction from the experiences of these last years: life is not a joke nor an entertainment; life is not even pleasure. Life is a heavy labor. Renunciation, constant renunciation—that is its secret meaning. . . . When we are young we think that the freer we are the better and the further we will go. Youth can think like that, but it is shameful to comfort oneself with an illusion when the stern face of truth has at last looked one in the eyes."

In spirit and content both "Mumu" (1855) and "Postoyaly dvor" ("The Inn") (1856) might well have been included in *A Sportsman's Sketches*, so sharp is their picture of the adverse effects of serfdom. "Mumu" is based on actual events that occurred at Spasskoe when Turgenev's mother, Varvara Petrovna, was still alive. Its two basic episodes highlight the inhumane treatment that serfs could be subjected to by a capricious and all-powerful landowner. A rich but miserly old widow is living out her dreary days in a large house on the outskirts of Moscow, looked after by numerous household serfs whom she has brought with her from the country. Of these the most remarkable is Gerasim, a man of powerful physique but deaf and dumb since birth. An enthusiastic worker at the country estates, he was at first reluctant to be brought to the town as a porter, but he had no choice. Gradually, however, he grows accustomed to his new life, even though he considers it pointless, and becomes as efficient at it as he had been on the land. One day the widow decides that two of her servants should get married. The groom is absolutely terrified—not of marriage, or of the widow, but of Gerasim, because he knows of his great strength, his temper, and that he is fond of the prospective bride himself. On the other hand, the girl meekly submits to her fate because she knows that the widow's power over her is unlimited. The other servants plot how best to reconcile the widow's orders with the fearsome anger it will provoke in Gerasim. Knowing Gerasim's antipathy to drunkenness, especially in women, they talk the girl into getting drunk, which she does. The sight of her has the desired effect on Gerasim, and he discards her. The young couple then marry and are dispatched to a distant estate. The story might well end there, but Turgenev introduces another episode. Some time after the departure of the newlyweds Gerasim rescues a drowning puppy spaniel called Mumu, from the river, and they become devoted to each other. The widow catches sight of Mumu and orders her brought into the house. Mumu immediately dislikes her and snaps at her. The widow orders her removed from the household, and that is done without Gerasim's knowledge. Later Mumu returns to Gerasim, and he conceals her from the widow, knowing full well the consequences if the dog is discovered. One morning, however, the widow hears Mumu whining and orders her destroyed. Gerasim takes Mumu himself and drowns her in the very river from which he had first rescued her. He then departs for the estate from which he came originally and continues to serve the widow faithfully despite her actions.

Such a story could have been very sentimental, but such is Turgenev's skill at understatement that this danger is averted. But there could be no clearer indictment of the power of a landowner over the serfs and the selfish nature of the exercise of that power. Yet, as in *A Sportsman's Sketches*, Turgenev never preaches or makes his criticism of the system overt. He states the facts and lets his readers draw their own conclusions.

"The Inn" is a longer and somewhat more complex story than "Mumu." Turgenev considered it in some respects better than any of the *Sportsman's Sketches* because he felt he had gone directly to the mark with it, and also could devote more time to it, as he had no thought of immediate publication. A serf, Akim, the owner of an inn, marries a young domestic servant who soon falls in love with a traveling salesman. He persuades her to steal Akim's savings to enable them to buy the inn from the landowner (some contemporary critics doubted whether this would have been possible, but Turgenev was quite correct since a serf's property remained legally that of the serf owner just as much as he did himself). Akim goes off on a frenzied drinking spree and then tries to set fire to the inn, but is apprehended. He is released on condition that he forgive his wife and the salesman. With remarkable humility he accepts his fate and becomes a pious pilgrim who wanders over Russia living on charity.

Both "Mumu" and "The Inn" can be seen as examples of the admirable quiet submission of the Russian peasant to his unhappy lot. This is an uncommonly Slavophile view for Turgenev. While agreeing with the opinion of Ivan Aksakov that Gerasim personified the mass of the Russian people with its terrifying strength and inscrutable humility, who would in time raise their voice but for the moment remained deaf and dumb, Turgenev was unhappy at the praise heaped upon "The Inn" from Slavophile quarters. He wrote to Annenkov on 2 April 1853 that he did not intend to depict the dispossessed Akim's later way of life as a model for the Russian peasant. He did not believe that the peasants would be saved by their purity of spirit and their saintliness, nor that these qualities would lead, as the Slavophiles suggested, to the humbling of the proud and the removal of evil, and thus save society. He admired Akim, but his way was not the way of all the peasants. Yet here again Turgenev left solutions to others.

Although it has an unnecessarily complicated plot and rather too many characters, "Yakov Pasynkov" (1855) is interesting for its depiction of the eponymous hero and for its development of Turgenev's ideas at the time. Turgenev displays an affection for his hero that is not to be repeated until *Fathers and Sons*. The prototype for Pasynkov was undoubtedly Belinsky, although many have seen Stankevich in him as well. He is poor, in ill health, and clumsy, yet he is the closest thing to a saint that Turgenev ever created: "On his lips the words 'the good,' 'the true,' 'life, learning, love,' however exultantly they were pronounced, never sounded false." In his presence it was impossible for anyone to lie; he is a transparently sincere, gentle, and honest man. He is also religious, a rare trait in Turgenev's heroes. Modest and unassuming, he never pushes himself forward even if it means losing the woman he loves to another. All these are the qualities Turgenev admitted he admired in Belinsky and Stankevich. What matters most in human life is not so much what you achieve but how you behave and what you are. This does not lead to happiness, but then in Turgenev's view happiness is not something that humanity can expect to attain.

While Turgenev was struggling to finish *Home of the Gentry*, he began to write "Asya," completing it in Rome in November 1857. It is one of his gentlest and most interesting love stories; the manuscript version shows that he devoted particular care to its writing. Despite the views of contemporary radical critics, it has little in the way of a moral and even less of a social message. This uncomplicated story of an unhappy love is set in a small village on the Rhine. The narrator, N. N., a middle-aged Russian, recalls events of twenty years ago, when he was on holiday and met the painter Gagin, who introduces him to his sister Asya. Gagin and N. N. become friends although the latter thinks the former only a dilettante. On one occasion, when Gagin says that if he has enough patience he will become someone, but if not then he will remain a half-educated scion of the gentry, Gagin clearly thinks it will be the latter, in an emblem of the fate of the Russian gentry as a whole. As N. N. gets to know the enigmatic, moody, self-conscious but attractive Asya better, he suspects that she is Gagin's mistress, but later Gagin tells him that she is in fact his illegitimate half-sister, whom he has brought up since the death of her parents when she was nine. Asya worships Gagin but has fallen in love with N. N. Although fascinated by her, when N. N. is told by Gagin of Asya's feelings he balks at the idea of marriage. When Asya declares her love, N. N. remains noncommital, but the following day he discovers that she and Gagin have left for Russia. Asya writes to him that things could have been so different if only he had said one word of encouragement to her, and N. N. realizes that he has let slip perhaps his only chance of happiness. However, perhaps Asya was more fortunate than she realized, for N. N.'s feelings prove shallow, and he "he didn't grieve over her for long." The theme of love and happiness lost through weakness in the man's character is common in Turgenev's fiction, but in "Asya" it is rather more the characterization of Gagin and especially of Asya herself that lends the story its lasting charm. While Turgenev himself saw "Asya" as just another story, albeit among his best, Chernyshevsky viewed it quite differently in his article "A Russian at the Rendezvous." He saw N. N. as typical of the vacuous men of the 1840s who were incapable of any action because of their social background. This interpretation is not indefensible, but it clearly does not coincide with Turgenev's intent.

Many of Turgenev's works contain an autobiographical element, but "First Love" was his most autobiographical story. Written and published in 1860, it contains among other things a description of his strong-willed and philandering father who possesses an ability to dominate women quite inaccessible to Turgenev.

In "First Love" the sixteen-year-old narrator, Volodya, falls in love with the enchanting and flirtatious Zinaida, who is four years older than he. Surrounded by a dubious circle of friends, she is staying with her mother in the house next to the narrator's. Gradually and painfully Volodya discovers that she is carrying on an affair with his cold and yet fascinating father. The story contrasts the ardent, almost innocent, love of the narrator with Zinaida's more mature, passionate, and tragic love, and is the clearest example in all of Turgenev's stories of the impossibility of successful love between the sexes. However rewarding and enriching the experience of love might be, it happens only once and for a short time, and life thereafter is no more than a postscript to it. "Beware the love of a woman," the narrator's father writes him, "that ecstasy . . . that poison." Neither Zinaida, the narrator, nor his father finds lasting pleasure in their relationship, and moreover the father dies shortly afterward from a stroke while Zinaida later marries but dies in childbirth. As a critic has pointed out, the news of Zinaida's death disturbs Volodya with a "profound and complex emotion; in part poignant regret for the irrevocable past, in part sad surprise that he feels her loss so little [although, it might be interposed, for different reasons altogether from those of N. N. in *Asya*]— how transitory, it comes home to him, are the most intense emotions—but predominantly bewildered, terrified awe at the precariousness of the human situation when seen in the light of death."[1]

Later in life Turgenev is supposed to have said that the only one of his stories that he reread with pleasure was "First Love." All the others, he said, contained things that were invented, but in "First Love" he described actual events without the least adornment. He added that when he read it he saw the characters as if alive before him.

Chapter Four
The First Three Novels and "Hamlet and Don Quixote"

Introduction

When it became clear in the early 1850s that Turgenev was moving toward the novel form, many of his contemporaries were apprehensive. They saw him as a master of the short story, a writer of delicate feeling, and keen, sometimes ironic, observation, a painter of unsurpassed literary portraits, a telling commentator on the social and human problems of landowner and peasant, and a competent dramatist. But his talent was that of a miniaturist. Contemporaries doubted his ability at writing on a larger scale. They were also aware that the history of the novel in Russia was relatively short, and that history would provide him with few appropriate models in either form or content. There had been hints in the eighteenth century of what would come later, but very few of the social and psychological themes and little of the Russian subject matter that marked the great novels of the following century and that contemporary critics were already demanding. Fedor Emin had written largely adventure stories having little to do with his native country, and even though Mikhail Chulkov's unfinished *Prigozhaya Povarikha* (*The Comely Cook*), a historical tale of the period just after the Battle of Poltava in 1709, is set in Russia, it is clearly modeled on Defoe's *Moll Flanders*. Nikolay Karamzin's short story "Bednaya Liza," ("Poor Liza"), his *Pisma russkogo puteshestvennika* (*Letters of a Russian Traveler*), although closer to popular eighteenth-century travel literature than to the novel, and especially his "Rytsar nashego vremeni" ("A knight of our time") are all nearer to the source of the Russian nineteenth-century novel. The traditional starting point, however, is Vasily Narezhny's satirical *Rossiysky Zhil Blas* (*A Russian Gil Blas*), parts of which were first published in 1814. Despite its obvious debt to Lesage, Narezhny was proud that it dealt with a Russian man in a Russian setting, but his clumsy style and rambling narrative technique meant that the novel was little read and that its influence on subsequent writers was negligible. From 1829 onward there appeared a flood of historical novels inspired by Walter Scott, the most notable being Mikhail Zagoskin's *Yury Miloslavsky* and the many by Ivan Lazhechnikov, all of which were remarkably popular although of no great literary merit. Arguably the best of the early Russian novelists, although he is largely forgotten today, was Aleksandr Bestuzhev-Marlinsky: his style was flamboyant but he had a verbal imagination and a skill with narration and dialogue that make him far superior to any of his contemporaries. None of these writers, though, had much influence on those who succeeded them, and Turgenev thought them all outmoded.

This was certainly not the case with his more immediate predecessors, Pushkin, Lermontov, and Gogol. But Pushkin's only completed "novel," *Eugene Onegin,* was written in verse, and Lermontov's *Geroy nashego vremeni* (*A Hero of our Time*) is more a cycle of short stories aimed at the gradual revelation of the psychology of its "hero" Pechorin than a novel as usually understood. With Gogol's *Mertvye dushi* (*Dead Souls,* 1842), however, the Russian novel came of age. Gogol was followed by a succession of writers of prose fiction: Dostoyevski, Herzen, Goncharov, Grigorovich, Turgenev himself, and then Tolstoy. Yet by the early 1850s of these only Herzen and Goncharov had published anything that can strictly speaking be called a novel. In 1847 the former published his *Kto vinovat?* (*Who is to blame?*) and the latter *Obyknovennaya istoriya* (*An Ordinary Story*), neither of which provided a model of artistic form.

Given the idiosyncratic development of the novel in Russia and Turgenev's supposed talents at the time, the concern of his contemporaries over the new turn of his writing was understandable. It is also clear that Turgenev himself, never the most self-confident of authors, had serious doubts about whether he could write novels. He even wondered whether the novel form would satisfy the demands of both Russian society and the reading public of his day, not to mention his own growing conviction that an author must describe and explain the main features of contemporary society in the hope that his readers would then have a clearer understanding of what was taking place in their midst. Only in such a way, Turgenev believed, could an author be useful to his country.

If indeed the novel was to be his genre, then what precise form should it take? He considered what he saw as the Walter Scott type of historical novel to be impossible in the Russia of the late 1840s because it no longer met the demands or the needs of society. Without elaborating, he saw more hope in the example of George Sand or Dickens, although he worried that perhaps Russian life had not yet reached a stage where any serious novel discussing Russian society was possible. Probably drawing on his own experience, he thought that certain types of expanded literary sketches were the most suitable form to employ. So he persevered with shorter works while he tried to solve his problems. On 2 April 1851 he wrote to a correspondent that, in addition to everything else, he was planning to devote himself to "a large work which I shall write *con amore* and at my leisure—without any *arrières- pensées* about the censorship." He obtained that leisure, albeit forced, with his arrest and exile to Spasskoe. He told Pauline Viardot in May 1852 that he could now devote himself to his "novel" with greater freedom because "I won't have to expose it to the clutches of the censorship." Yet five months later he had still not started, and it took a letter from his great friend Annenkov to force him to face up to the problem again. Replying from Spasskoe on 28 October 1852, Turgenev thanked Annenkov for encouraging him not to give up his writing and perhaps try something new. "Everything you say," Turgenev wrote,

is an undisputed truth. I feel it as deeply as you and I subscribe to every word. I must travel a new path—I must find one and bid farewell forever to my old style. I tried to extract from my characters drawn from the ordinary people their basic essences— *triples extraits*—and then put them into little bottles, saying, as it were, uncork them, honored reader, and sniff—don't you sense a truly Russian type? But enough of that, enough! The question remains, though, am I able to do anything on a larger scale? Will I be able to draw in clear and simple lines? I don't know the answer and I never shall unless I try. But believe me, you'll hear something new from me—or nothing ever again. . . . Yet something will come from me if only I can destroy the literary man in me.

Taking his own words to heart, he tried again. He called his new work *Dva pokoleniya* (*Two Generations*); by the following February he had completed seven chapters of a planned twelve, which, he told Annenkov, ran to about 500 manuscript pages. He soon became dissatisfied with it and burned most of the manuscript. When a short extract was published a few years later, it passed largely unnoticed by the critics and met with only partial and grudging praise from his friends. From the extract ("The Privy Office") and from other sources[1] it can be seen what at least the first part of the novel was to have described. It is set in the country, on the estate of a rich landowner, Glafira Ivanovna, a strong-willed, eccentric, inconsistent despot with little regard for other people. She trusts only one person, a neighbor, Chermak, clearly intended to be one of the main characters. A measure of gaiety is brought to the unhappy home by the arrival of a young tutor, Elizaveta Mikhaylovna, a charming and graceful girl who knows her own mind. She contrasts so strongly with everyone else there that she has a marked effect on all of them, not least on Glafira's weak and capricious twenty-six-year-old son, Dmitry Petrovich. After falling easily in love with her, he later grows to hate her. We do not know how Turgenev would have developed the story, whether it would have turned out more a psychological study, as might be deduced from what is known of it, or a social one (the title is open to either interpretation), but Turgenev told Annenkov that he wanted to describe as simply and honestly as he could what he himself had experienced both on his mother's estate and on those of her neighbors. Yet the impression remains that the work might well have emerged as little more than an amalgam of characters and plots taken from his earlier stories and plays, and hardly "something new."

Clearly Turgenev found the writing of his "large work" difficult, unsatisfying, and at the time ultimately impossible. By the end of 1853 he seems to have abandoned the idea altogether. It has been suggested that he had not, until 1855 when he wrote *Rudin*, sufficiently deepened his understanding of human nature and society, of human destiny and the world of nature to embark upon a "large work," one "large" not merely in terms of length.[2] That he had not until *Rudin* found a sufficiently important theme or interesting enough characters through whom to express it is perhaps the main reason for his abandoning *Two Generations*. Other critics[3] have suggested that Turgenev took so long to produce his first novel for more personal reasons, despite what he himself might have said on the matter, for he was usually too irresolute and always too mercurial to wish to expend the effort necessary to write a novel unless continually prompted and encouraged. Furthermore, in the Russia of the 1850s the novel had to deal with social questions, and Turgenev disliked treating such problems at length in his fiction. "I am not politically active," he wrote to his confidante Countess Lambert in May 1863. "I never did and I never shall occupy myself with politics; it is alien to me and uninteresting and I pay attention to it only insofar as it is necessary for a writer who has been called upon to paint pictures of contemporary life." But was he really "called upon," or did he choose this path? Furthermore, Turgenev *was* interested in politics then, and remained so all his life, even though he was never, despite what the czarist authorities may have suspected from time to time, a political activist. Perhaps, finally, Turgenev really did doubt whether he possessed the necessary skills to write "something new," something "large." Indeed, he never succeeded in describing complicated mental conditions, nor were his plots ever anything other than straightforward. Both these facts would tend to prevent a man as tentative as Turgenev from turning to the novel. But he did. Whatever the ultimate reasons for the length of time it took him to write his first novel, he actually produced it in a remarkably short time, and it did deal, at least in part, with a social and relatively contemporary theme.

Rudin

For Russia 1855 was, as Turgenev himself might have expresed it, a climacteric year. The thirty-year reign of Nicholas I, a period of strict military and autocratic rule, of increasing centralization and bureaucracy, of repression and relative economic stagnation—and of harsh literary censorship—had ended in January with the czar's death. The picture Nicholas had tried to draw of a strong, well-governed, and prosperous country, with little or no internal dissent, and whose armies were the pride of Europe, faded rapidly as the fortunes of war in the Crimea went increasingly against Russia. The accession of Alexander II brought with it a new atmosphere, favorable to hopes for change. One observer noted that "it seemed as if out of a depressing dark dungeon we were emerging, if not into God's light, at least into an antechamber where we could sense refreshing air."[4] Yet this unaccustomed freedom with its accompanying expectation of real reform released forces that neither the new czar nor his government would be able ultimately to contain, and Alexander, the czar-liberator, in the end died at the hand of a political assassin. During the late 1850s and afterward the Russian nobility—the landowning class, the owners of most of the country's wealth, and also the only educated section of society—found its long-established supremacy challenged by a younger generation of different upbringing and different aspirations. These young radicals owed no allegiance to Russia's traditions, had no interest, economic or social, in the institution of serfdom, and despised political liberalism, which they considered halfhearted and ineffective. Furthermore, they challenged traditional opinions on art and in particular established notions on the role of the writer in society. While Herzen, who had left for exile in Western Europe in 1847, became the leading Russian publicist of the 1850s, the journal *Contemporary* would express in its pages many of the new ideas being discussed inside the country. Although edited by Nekrasov and Panaev, both men of Turgenev's own generation of the 1840s, it soon came under the guiding hand of Chernyshevsky, whose materialist and radical ideas appealed to the younger generation of the 1860s and fundamentally upset people like Turgenev, who found themselves increasingly alienated from them. Although there were also more personal reasons involved, it was basically this change in emphasis that led Turgenev to sever all connections with *Contemporary* after the 1850s.[5] But in 1855 this was still in the future, and Turgenev, as sensitive as anyone to the changes taking place in his country, realized at the time that Russia had reached a watershed and that he as a writer had a duty to examine it. He wanted to assess the role of his own generation to see whether it could justly be called ineffective, whether it could accurately be blamed for the current state of the nation. Although in some respects in his novels he acted as a historian of the Russian intelligentsia, he was also its critic. This is apparent from his very first novel, even if we agree that Turgenev failed to solve the problem of integrating his social and political commentary with its love story.

The final impetus for actually writing the novel after all the prevarications of previous years was probably provided by a visit to Spasskoe by three of his friends, who convinced him that it was his duty to his country to write his novel. The four spent most of the time completing and producing a short play, "Shkola gostepriimstva" ("The School for Hospitality"). This helps to explain why *Rudin* strikes many readers as rather theatrical in its construction, with each chapter resembling a "scene" and dialogue moving the action along. The first draft was done in June and July 1855, when Turgenev was forced to stay within the confines of Spasskoe by an outbreak of cholera, and then taken to Moscow in October, when Turgenev made some changes in the wake of certain events and adverse comments from his friends. It appeared the following year in *Contemporary* and soon afterward as a book.

The setting for the novel is the country estate of Darya Mikhaylovna Lasunskaya; the main action takes place over a period of about two months. The plot is extremely simple. Into this settled, provincial backwater falls a stranger, Dmitry Rudin, who powerfully affects the lives of all the local residents, and especially the daughter of the household, Natalya. When he leaves things quickly revert to their former placid state, but some of the individuals find their lives changed forever. The novel's interest does not therefore lie in the story as such, but rather in the various characters, their psychological conflicts, and the sociological questions Turgenev examines.

The novel opens with a description of Alexandra Lipina, a widow, childless, and reasonably wealthy, who stops on the way home to bring comfort to a dying peasant woman. This might well have been the start of one of the *Sportsman's Sketches*, but here the peasants play no further role in the story, and in this episode they only illustrate Alexandra's benevolent and philanthropic nature. This device not only immediately establishes facets of her personality and places her in a definite social class, but also enables Turgenev to introduce many other characters either directly or through conversations. The reader meets the staid, worthy, but weak-willed Sergey Volyntsev, her unmarried brother who looks after her estates; Mikhaylo Lezhnev, a neighboring landowner; Konstantin Pandalevsky, a rather disreputable hanger-on on the estate; and finally Basistov, a young student employed as tutor to Darya Mikhaylovna's two young sons. Pandalevsky was originally to have had a larger role in the novel as Anna Pavlovna's suitor and thus provide a parallel to the relationship between Rudin and Natalya, but Turgenev abandoned this idea.

At this stage the two leading female characters, Darya Mikhaylovna and Natalya, are only mentioned in conversation. In introducing new characters Turgenev commonly first gives a physical description of them, their age, their appearance, and sometimes provides a little prehistory. Less commonly they are described by other characters. Certain aspects of their personalities, also revealed in this way, are later reinforced through dialogue. This method of portraiture ensures that the characters, however minor, come sharply into focus when they appear. It is an artistic method markedly different from, for example, that of Tolstoy, who achieves his effects by a steady accumulation of small details, often apparently but hardly ever in fact insignificant. Turgenev wrote novels on a far less expansive scale than Tolstoy, and his method, although simple and straightforward, is adequate for his purposes.

Having established the general setting, as Turgenev regularly does, and introduced a number of characters (although none of those who are to play a major role has yet physically appeared), Turgenev in chapter 2 moves the scene inside the house, where most of the action will take place, and then introduces other members of the household: the socially and intellectually pretentious Darya Mikhaylovna, her children, their French governess Mlle Boncourt, and the mysogynistic poseur Afrikan Pigasov, whose sarcasm and definite opinions on everything from art and literature to scientific progress pass for wit in the limited environment of the country estate. Of all the characters, Pigasov and Darya Mikhaylovna are described in the most detail, Lezhnev and Natalya in the least. At the very end of the chapter, after the excitement felt by all the household at the expected arrival for dinner of an important guest has been skillfully described, a servant announces Rudin's completely unexpected advent. This became a typical constructional device of Turgenev's novels: The arrival of a stranger in an established, settled environment—Rudin here, Lavretsky in *Home of the Gentry*, Insarov in *On the Eve*, Bazarov in *Fathers and Sons*. The stranger will always differ notably from the other characters, especially the heroine, in both education and background, but also psychologically, because Turgenev's novels all incorporate love stories. Yet they are never the stories of a hero and heroine similar to each other in either upbringing or personality. Contrast provides the moving force behind much of what happens, and this device, apparent from the very first of the *Sportsman's Sketches*, is frequently employed by Turgenev in dealing with the impact of the new and the different and the tensions they create. The obverse is true with Litvinov in *Smoke* and Nezhdanov in *Virgin Soil* because, although they are strangers in the location where the action takes place, it is their own ideas, rather than those of others, that are challenged.

Once Rudin has arrived the succeeding chapters divide into two groups: 3–5 and 6–11, with a time lapse of two months in between. They gradually reveal his personality, which is the novel's main purpose. Chapter 12, which takes place some two years later, is an epilogue informing us that, after Rudin's departure, Alexandra has married Lezhnev and they have a baby son; Pigasov has aged but grown no wiser, Natalya and Volyntsev are man and wife, and Darya Mikhaylovna and Pandalevsky continue as before. We learn that Rudin has been abroad, behaving very much as he did during his brief visit, and is now roaming aimlessly around Russia. Yet Turgenev clearly felt that if he ended the novel there his hero would still not be fully depicted. In 1860, four years after the novel's original publication, he added a specific epilogue describing Rudin's life in the few years after the main action. We shall discuss below whether this does in fact help us understand this complex man and the environment that produced him, but certain of Turgenev's contemporaries thought it had changed the novel for the worse, and considered the new ending unsatisfactory in the extreme.

The construction of *Rudin* may be faulted for its unevenness and for its rather episodic flow. The first two chapters set the scene; the next three concentrate on the hero's arrival and the more positive aspects of his personality; there is then a gap during which Natalya falls in love with Rudin. Many readers find this gap a great weakness in the novel, for Turgenev thus does not delineate Natalya's personality sufficiently, using her primarily as a means to reveal the character of Rudin. This would be acceptable in those characters who remain minor throughout, but when the heroine of a love story is involved this is surely a serious fault. Chapters 6–11 form a contrast to the preceding three in that they show other, less positive, sides to Rudin and his ultimate departure from the estate in disgrace. The novel concludes in effect with two epilogues. This sectionalized construction leads to the conclusion that Turgenev at the time he wrote *Rudin* was not fully in control of the techniques of the novel and was still thinking in terms of the short story. Such deficiencies in construction, and particularly in the portrayal of the heroine, were eliminated in his second and subsequent novels.

The picture Turgenev wished to draw of his central character was meant to arouse sympathy for a certain type of intellectual whom Turgenev thought typical of his own generation, but a critical sympathy. Rudin was modeled on several individuals whom Turgenev knew, especially on Mikhail Bakunin,

though not Bakunin the later anarchist but the young Bakunin, the man
Turgenev remembered from his student days in Berlin when they were both
under the influence of German romantic philosophy. Certain of Bakunin's
positive characteristics emerge in the portrait of Rudin—his striking ability
to talk and to inspire others—and also some negative traits: his wish to dominate others and organize their lives for them, his habit of borrowing money
and generally living at other people's expense. All these were present in
Rudin of the manuscript Turgenev took with him to Moscow in the fall of
1855. Just at that time, however, Bakunin had been arrested in Austria, de-
ported to Russia, and imprisoned. Turgenev felt it necessary to make his central fictional character less obviously based upon his old friend. Furthermore,
one of the most revered and respected men of his own generation, Timofey
Granovsky (who incidentally thought the young Turgenev "light-weight and
lacking in character"), had just died. Turgenev had known and admired him
in the 1840s and wanted to include more of Granovsky's idealism and altruism in his final portrait of Rudin. Consequently some changes were made.
Most important, Turgenev added what is now chapter 6, containing a description by Lezhnev of his university days with Rudin in Moscow and their
mutual experiences, especially in the Pokorsky circle. Certain elements of
Bakunin's character incorporated in Rudin are counterbalanced by others
from Pokorsky, generally regarded as Turgenev's portrait of Stankevich and
his tribute to him as the leader of the most influential student circle of the
1830s. Turgenev contrasts Bakunin's superficial brilliance with the inspira-
tional genius of Stankevich. Rudin possesses both of these. Still, whoever the
prototypes for him were, and whatever Turgenev's intentions, the finished
portrait stands on its own.

When Rudin first enters the Lasunskaya household we are told he is
"about thirty-five, tall, a little round-shouldered, swarthy, with irregular but
expressive and intelligent features and a liquid brilliance in his lively deep-
blue eyes." His clothes are not new, and rather tight, as if he had outgrown
them. Immediately Turgenev begins to establish his personality. Rudin's verbal destruction of the opinions, or rather prejudices, of the cynical Pigasov
demonstrates his eloquence, his shining idealism, his ability to persuade people of the truth of what he is saying even if some of them are not sure of the
meaning of his words. Men must have vision, they must put their faith in
knowledge, they must understand the needs and desires of their fellowmen,
they must serve their country and humanity at large. Rudin wins the victory
over Pigasov, yet it is a victory tinged with pessimism, for at the end of the
first evening Rudin acknowledges that despite what he has said and fervently
believes, all human accomplishment is nevertheless ephemeral. Little by little

Turgenev fills out the portrait with rather less admirable traits of Rudin's personality. He is rather touchy, and seems embarrassed by any reference to his former life or inquiries about his future plans. He has no sense of humor nor of the ridiculous in life. He can talk brilliantly and listen attentively, but he cannot converse. He has no compunction about borrowing money and apparently little regard for the necessity of repayment. His deep sincerity and rigid but limited sense of duty force him into errors of judgment. His grasp of ideas is firm, but his persistent intellectualizing and introspection have deprived him of the ability to understand others or consider their feelings. In the intellectual sphere he has no equal, but his ability to cope on the emotional level is correspondingly retarded. In this respect he bears a marked similarity to both Pushkin's Eugene Onegin and Lermontov's Pechorin. Of all the facets of the human personality, Onegin displays the primacy of the aesthetic, Pechorin that of the will. With Rudin it is the intellect.[6] In all three cases other aspects, especially the emotional, suffer in varying degrees. Onegin can only respond to Tatyana as the married, sophisticated society lady she becomes, while Pechorin uses women to satisfy his pride, with little or no concern for their reactions to his machinations. Rudin subordinates the emotions to the point where they rise to the surface only very briefly and all human relationships are beyond him except on the intellectual plane.

When Rudin first asks Natalya whether she has ever been in love and the impressionable young girl is naturally at a loss for words, Rudin at once begins to pontificate, to analyze the emotion, to question it, and to wonder whether it is tragic. He does this without any concern for the effect this will have upon the spontaneous and honest Natalya. When later Rudin realizes that Natalya has indeed fallen in love with him, he begins to examine the emotion again, as well as his own motives. Love to Rudin is yet another intellectual phenomenon to be analyzed, but when he confronts it in reality he cannot cope with it. This has its parallel in the occasion when in effect he asks Volyntsev for his permission to court Natalya, knowing full well that Volyntsev is in love with her himself. He cannot understand why Volyntsev reacts with amazement, embarrassment, and hostility. Rudin's inability even to consider, let alone to understand, the reaction of others and their opinions of him emerges again when Natalya, impressed by his fine words, asks him at one point how he plans to put these words into effect. Visibly shaken by the question, he merely agrees that it is disgraceful that he has achieved nothing at his age, but argues that this seems to be his fate. When at their final meeting Natalya asks Rudin what she should do in view of the fact that Pandalevsky had overheard one of their more intimate conversations, when Natalya even suggested she was ready to elope, and had reported the matter

to her mother, he replies that she should submit to her mother. While
Natalya is heartbroken by his rejection of her love, his fatalism was something she neither expected nor could accept. But his course of meek submission applies as much to himself as to her. He knows that Natalya's mother
will not allow the relationship to continue, and this releases him from any ob-
ligation toward her.

Turgenev's Rudin is ultimately a failure. Rudin is a man of brilliant and
exciting qualities, intellectually sharp and extremely talented; he enraptures
the household into which he accidentally enters with his ideas and his ideals;
he has tremendous potential, but a potential that remains unfulfilled. Rudin
is incapable of action when it is demanded, not only on the emotional but
even on the physical level. He is basically heartless; he is vain, boastful, and
inconsiderate; he is incapable of achieving anything in his own life. If the
novel ended after he admits the impossibility of returning Natalya's love,
Rudin would be a generally unsympathetic character, a further example of
the type of superfluous man Turgenev depicted in Rakitin (*A Month in the
Country*) or Chulkaturin ("The Diary of a Superfluous Man") or the eponymous "Hamlet of Shchigrovsky District." The reader's reaction to him would
be as negative as that of the majority of the characters in the novel whose lives
he briefly touches. Yet even before he added the epilogue Turgenev clearly
wanted Rudin to differ from his comparable predecessors. In the farewell letter to Natalya Turgenev grants Rudin a touch of genuine sincerity and self-
knowledge that endows him with something of the tragic nature of a real
"superfluous man" of the 1840s. He may be a failure himself, but those who
follow him may be more successful when the time is ripe. In Turgenev's view
the period of the 1840s was clearly not ripe for decisive action in the social or
political sphere in Russia. Perhaps the effect of Rudin's words on the young
Basistov gives hope for the future, however vaguely that hope is expressed.

Certain adverse responses to *Rudin* on its publication and Turgenev's own
doubts about whether he had succeeded in fully delineating Rudin's character led to the addition of the epilogue. Here Lezhnev, whom Turgenev had
used earlier as both a mouthpiece for his own ideas and as the man who helps
explain, albeit with little enthusiasm, Rudin's personality, meets him again
after some years. Rudin has aged considerably in appearance and is still emotionally reticent although, as we might expect, he welcomes Lezhnev's invita-
tion to dinner. The pair discuss old times in a mood of mutual friendliness,
and Rudin then describes what has happened to him in the intervening years.
He had tried unsuccessfully to manage an estate, then had joined forces with
a businessman in an attempt to make a river navigable and thus derive a for-
tune from trade, but that enterprise failed too. Finally, he had become a

teacher but had lost his job because of petty jealousies and because he did not keep to the rules. Now Rudin has arrived at a sense of his own failure, realizing that everything he has preached with so much conviction was only words. Lezhnev sees a broken man: his speech has lost its fire, his eyes have lost their lustre, and everything about him "expressed an ultimate exhaustion of spirit, a secret and unspoken misery." The reader can now understand him better, and begins to sympathize with his predicament as his portrait is filled out and softened. Rudin departs with only death awaiting him. At the very end of the epilogue Turgenev takes the story to a precise historical moment. On 26 June 1848 Rudin is on the barricades in Paris at the time of the revolution. He is shot through the heart—after the revolution has failed.

The cogency of this conclusion is open to some doubt. It does recall Rudin's earlier statement that he would probably end by dying for a cause in which he did not believe, but the fact that the cause was already lost anyway makes his death even more meaningless. If Turgenev wished to show that the type of Russian of the 1840s whom he had portrayed in Rudin was indeed capable of action beyond "saying the right word at the right moment," then this conclusion points to his view that the time for such a hero had not arrived in Russia itself. Rudin dies fighting for a foreign cause, on foreign soil. Ultimately he is even deprived of his nationality: "'Tiens,' said one of the fleeing insurgents to another, 'on vient de tuer le Polonais.'" That Pole was Dmitry Rudin.

Home of the Gentry

When the Russian government announced its intention to emancipate the peasants, it became clear to everyone that their lives would undergo significant change. Turgenev was in Rome at the end of 1857 when he heard that Czar Alexander had formally ordered the drafting of the necessary legislation, a step that meant that its subsequent promulgation was inevitable. Although he thought himself financially secure enough not to fear any deterioration in his standard of living, he began seriously to wonder what other men in his position might actually do under the changed social conditions. Conscious of his own lack of purpose, he concluded that all men, especially those of his own social class, would be called upon to specialize in spheres best suited to their particular capabilities. He thought he would transform himself into an active "landowner" rather than an "estate owner" who left the management of his properties to other people. This, however, was a passing phase: perhaps he failed to convince himself in the matter. He worried continually that his real talent was not for farming, with all its responsibilities, and even less, he wrote, for the army or the bureaucracy, which seemed the only other options open to him, but for writing, and especially writing for useful social purposes. This talent, he thought, was being wasted. As he approached his fortieth birthday in 1858 he opined that his first youth (and his second) had passed, and that it was high time he decided where his life was leading and what he should be doing with it. "I can be nothing if not a writer," he wrote to Annenkov on 1 December 1857, "but up until now I have been only a dilettante. In the future that will change."

It is not surprising, therefore, that Turgenev started planning his second novel, *Home of the Gentry*, as soon as he had finished *Rudin*: his desire to devote himself to it entirely was an expression of his newfound determination. Yet this determination wavered continually, and the novel remained incomplete until he forced himself to finish it—rather quickly, as was his custom—in 1858. It was published early in the following year. In it he enlarged upon his hopes and fears for the immediate future, and expressed his nostalgia for what he saw as good in the former social arrangements, which would, he imagined, soon disappear. The novel is also his first unambiguous statement that a man's endeavors redeem him irrespective of whether they lead to anything tangible, that the Quixote type is preferable to the Hamlet. Because he was considering what he valued most in Russian traditions in *Home of the Gentry*, Turgenev was here at his most Russophile. This does not mean that he had abandoned his Westernist convictions, but he did emphasize the peculiarly Russian sides of his characters and looked quite critically at certain aspects of Western culture.

A strong hint of this Russophilism appears at the end of *Rudin*, when Lezhnev launches an attack upon cosmopolitanism, declaring it rubbish and the cosmopolitan a nonentity. Outside nationality there is no art, no truth, no life, nothing. "Russia," Lezhnev declares, "can get along without any of us, but none of us can get along without Russia. Woe to him who thinks he can, and double woe to him who actually does get on without her!" The root cause of Rudin's unhappiness, thinks Lezhnev, is that he does not know Russia at all. And that is a very great unhappiness. This view recurs in the story of the father of Lavretsky, the hero of *Home of the Gentry*. Lavretsky's father was a fervent Anglophile. Although that is not necessarily eccentric, many of his other convictions definitely were. He attempted to raise his son not as a Russian, but rather as a European. The main result of this was to make him rootless, neither Russian nor European. While Lavretsky, despite his upbringing and later life, ultimately recovers his roots in Russia, his father suddenly goes blind and wanders around Russia vainly seeking a cure before dying an ill-tempered Russian landowner of the old school. Turgenev's metaphor is clear.

On the other hand, what he considered the more positive sides of Russian life are exemplified in the life story of Lavretsky himself, his search for a "nest" and a purpose in life, and his love for the novel's heroine Liza Kalitina, in whose personality Turgenev incorporates much of what he thought most valuable in the human spirit.

As is his custom, Turgenev first sets the scene for the forthcoming action. The setting is not the country estate of *Rudin*, but the city house of the Kalitins in the town of O——— (a thinly disguised Orel, the place of Turgenev's birth). The purpose, though, is the same. For Turgenev the estate with its manor house (or here the substantial town residence) symbolizes stability in a world of change. It is a haven of peace that provides a sense of security far away from the bustle, concerns, and inconsequence of the outside world, yet also a place where the inhabitants can be confronted by new ideas or challenged about their accepted values and standards of thought and behavior. The challenges, though, always come from outside the confines of the house. The difference between *Home of the Gentry*, however, and *Rudin, On the Eve*, and *Fathers and Sons*, is that the outsider, Lavretsky, has returned rather to find himself and his "nest," and not to shake the other characters out of their complacency. Through nine chapters the reader is given far more direct information about Lavretsky than about any other of Turgenev's heroes. The manner in which it is introduced into the novel might be considered a fault in composition, as can the later introduction of minor characters who express a point of view and then play no further part in the story. This shows that Turgenev was still attempting to come to grips with the particular demands of the novel form. He was well aware of this himself, and apologized at the start of chapter 8 for breaking the thread of the narrative to provide the history of Lavretsky's unhappy life up until the moment of his reappearance in the town of O———. Then, at the end of chapter 16, he gently begs his reader to return with him to the main story.

As a young man Lavretsky had suffered from the willfulness of a father who had used him as an experimental subject for his ill-considered educational ideas. He marries an empty-headed, flirtatious woman who takes him to the vacuous world of European high society and soon leaves him for the superficial attractions of a Parisian dandy in but the first of many infidelities. Finally, it all proves too much for Lavretsky, and he returns without his wife to Russia, confused, embittered, but determined to justify his existence in his own eyes and those of others by useful activity. He is soon attracted to the nineteen-year-old Liza, whom he had known earlier when she was a young girl. When false news of his wife's death reaches him, his love for Liza deepens: he sees her spontaneity, sincerity, openness, and serious turn of mind as compensating for much of what he feels is lacking in his own personality. Yet—as is almost always the case with him—his apparently attainable ambitions founder on several obstacles. His love for Liza is thwarted by her strong religious convictions and, more immediately, by the news that his wife is in fact still alive. The two women in Lavretsky's life represent in many ways the extremes of Turgenev's female characters in general. His wife, Varvara Pavlovna, has no redeeming traits at all. She openly exploits Lavretsky at every opportunity, she is continually unfaithful to him and returns to him only when she needs him, and she is thoughtless, selfish, and uncaring. She makes his life a complete misery. She is the most vivid example in all Turgenev's fiction of the woman who finds a justification of her existence in exercising power over a man incapable of resisting it. In sharp contrast, Liza is the most religious, moral, strong-willed, and spiritual of all his heroines. She is seriously worried by the thought of loving a man who has been promised to another and takes the reappearance of his wife as a form of divine retribution for her audacity. She decides to spend the rest of her life as a nun in a remote convent in order to seek atonement. Her inner purity and her spiritual strength are displayed most movingly at the end of the novel. Some years after the main events have occurred, Lavretsky visits the convent. He watches as she silently passes by a few feet away from him, but "she did not look at him; only the lashes of the eye turned toward him fluttered very slightly and she dropped her emaciated face even lower, and the fingers of her clasped hands, entwined in a rosary, pressed more tightly together."

As in *Rudin*, the love story in *Home of the Gentry*—however movingly told and unhappily ended, however much more successfully incorporated into the main body of the narrative, however much more fully Turgenev describes the personalities of Lavretsky and Liza and their love for each other—is still but part of the whole. But Turgenev does reiterate his persistent belief that love between a man and a woman can never bring lasting happiness even though human life without it is impoverished. He also discusses more personal concerns, such as the primacy of duty in social life, the need for work and renunciation, the problems of dilettantism and specialization and how these best met the demands of Russian life at the time. Unlike Rudin, however, Lavretsky has an inner strength of character and knows what he would like to achieve. From his first appearance he is on the verge of action: "I shall plough the fields, as my grandfather did." Practical activity will give his ruined life new purpose, and devotion to a traditional occupation will restore his links with the past. But he finds it extremely difficult to take the next step. The ideal founders on the complexity of its realization. A visit from his impoverished university friend Mikhalevich highlights the problem for him.

Mikhalevich reminds Lavretsky of his former idealism. "Religion, progress, humanity," he shouts at him; and Lavretsky remembers. But he cannot immediately overcome his bitterness over his wife's behavior or the doubts into which he has since fallen. Mikhalevich accuses him of lapsing into the self-pity and apathy typical of his class. Although, like Rudin, Mikhalevich is a man of words and not action, his message is the same: "each of us has a duty, a great responsibility before God, the people and himself." This duty for people like Lavretsky, members of the landowning class and the intelligentsia, is to work for their country, not for themselves.

To transform words into action, however, is nearly as difficult for Lavretsky as it was for Rudin, and for Turgenev too. Lavretsky comes closest to a solution in chapter 33, during an exchange with Panshin. Expressing an opinion that Turgenev himself held for most of his life, Panshin suggests that reforms must be introduced from above to be successful. Lavretsky responds that this implies action by the older generation, and it has already been found wanting. Hope lies with the younger generation. Lavretsky praises "the youth and independence of Russia . . . for the new men, their convictions, their desires." Lavretsky further stresses "the impossibility of progress by leaps and bounds or of making high-handed changes from above through officialdom" because such changes, when they had been attempted before, were not supported by any real knowledge of Russia or its people, nor by any ideal. Lavretsky demands a recognition of Russia's own "popular 'truth' and reconciliation with it." To reach this goal we must have a clear ideal and a determination not to be sidetracked by other interests or considerations. To Panshin Lavretsky's faith in Russia's youth, the "new men," shows yet further irresponsibility on Lavretsky's part; he remains "an outmoded conservative."

The argument is continued in the conversation between Panshin and Lemm, both in their explicit disagreements and also in their personal antagonism. The handsome, sociable, and charming Panshin is a splendid horseman and writes music. But he also holds an influential position in the government, something Turgenev always viewed with the gravest suspicion and even, as here, a sign of moral failure. On the other hand, Lemm has none of Panshin's social accomplishments. The son of a poor German family, he is lonely, deprived, and unhappy. He is a poorly paid music teacher considered of no account by the society in which he is forced by circumstances to live. He is devoted to his music, and his compositions are far superior to any of Panshin's rather shallow efforts. But society does not recognize them, which upsets him deeply. He always comes off second-best in any encounter with Panshin, and yet Turgenev clearly prefers him to Panshin. He seems to suggest that Lemm's dedication to his art redeems a life of all too apparent failure. Panshin is merely a dilettante; consequently all his talents are superficial, and he will achieve nothing of value. What we are told of Lavretsky at the very end of the novel confirms this. His life throughout might well be considered unhappy and Lavretsky himself a failure, like Lemm, and Rudin before him. However, in the epilogue, set some eight years later, he has found a modicum of contentment. He has fulfilled his earlier vow to become a good landowner and has worked not only for himself: as far as was possible, he has done his best to ensure the livelihood of his peasants. It might not be anything extraordinary, but it is the only positive achievement of his life. Consequently, he has recovered those roots from which his upbringing alienated him. He has at last found his "nest."

Home of the Gentry was extremely popular both in Russia and abroad, among critics and readers alike. The fact that it is today probably the least read of his first four novels is regrettable. The stable environment in which the action takes place, the arrival of a stranger to disrupt it, the ineffectual hero and the stronger-willed heroine, their moving but unfulfilled love for each other, the well-delineated minor characters, the discussion of ideas and contemporary themes, the use of contrast as a stylistic device, the lucid and elegant style, the vividness of the nature descriptions, the author's obvious love of the countryside, his pessimism about the human condition and the possibility of lasting happiness, the nostalgia, the gentleness, and the ironic humor—all these things are Turgenev at his most characteristic.

On the Eve

The idea for what would become Turgenev's third published novel first occurred to him while he was in exile in Spasskoe, and more particularly during the Crimean War. A neighbor of his, before departing to join the Russian army, left him a notebook containing the outline of a story of a strong-willed, committed Russian girl and her love for a Bulgarian patriot. She goes to his country, but he soon dies. Thus the seeds of *On the Eve* were planted. When Turgenev had completed *Rudin* and *Home of the Gentry*, he returned to this story at the beginning of 1858, drawing up a list of characters and an outline of the plot. He settled down to serious writing at Vichy in France in the summer of the following year, and completed it quickly in Spasskoe in the fall. It was published in January 1860.

On the Eve is the story of Elena Stakhova, a Russian girl who falls in love with a Bulgarian revolutionary, Dmitry Insarov. At the time of their first meeting, just before the Crimean War, he is an exile in Russia studying at the university. Insarov is totally dedicated to freeing his native country from

Turkish occupation and this—in addition to making him the most Quixote-like of all of Turgenev's heroes—strikes a strong chord of sympathy in Elena, who finds no such strong ideals in the Russian men of her generation. She unites herself to Insarov and to his cause and leaves her admittedly uninspiring family and Russia knowing that she will probably never return. The relationship between Elena and Insarov, at first secret, blossoms into love and then marriage, but not before she has a premonition of his death as he suffers a serious illness. Insarov recovers from this first alarum but falls ill again, on the way back to Bulgaria, first in Vienna and then in Venice, where he dies. Elena takes his body on to his motherland, which then becomes hers and where she will participate in the insurrection in his place. Turgenev's meditation at novels' end on the meaning of death, especially when it happens to a young man, illustrates the problems of any attempt to ally his natural philosphical pessimism with the optimism of people like Insarov and Elena, people with an ideal and a goal in life in whom Turgenev could never entirely believe, however much he admired their dedication and strength of character.

On the Eve is larger in scope than either *Rudin* or *Home of the Gentry*. This is immediately apparent from the wider variety of locations in which the action takes place. While *Rudin* is set basically at the Lasunskaya country estate and *Home of the Gentry* in the Kalitins' town house in O———, here we are taken from Bersenev's rooms to the Stakhovs' Moscow residence, from Insarov's lodgings to the family summer dacha, and from Moscow to Vienna and on to Venice (of which city, incidentally, Turgenev provides a marvelous lyrical description). The story also encompasses a longer period of time than the two previous ones. Third, the narrative is less simple and of a piece, and consequently perhaps more loose. These differences also affect the methods of Turgenev's characterization. In the first two novels he had concentrated to all intents and purposes on the leading personages, on Rudin and to a lesser extent Natalya, and on Lavretsky and Liza. His numerous minor characters tended to exist only in relation to the major ones, to tell the reader about them rather than exist in their own right. But at the outset of *On the Eve* two of the minor characters, Bersenev and Shubin, are shown in far greater detail than any of their counterparts in *Rudin* or *Home of the Gentry*. In a lengthy conversation between them on the banks of the Moscow River Turgenev not only sketches their differing personalities but also introduces the main issues with which the novel will deal. Contrasted with Bersenev and Shubin, who represent the Russian younger generation, are Elena's parents, Anna and Nikolay Stakhov, upper class, set in their ways, strikingly unimaginative, whom

Turgenev portrays at best ironically. Elena herself is described fully only in chapter 6.

If we recall Turgenev's earlier artistic method of first setting the scene for the action and then introducing characters who are to play lesser roles before the major participant appears, we might assume that the main focus in *On the Eve* will be, not on Bersenev, Shubin, or even Elena, but on Insarov, who first enters in chapter 7. This was probably Turgenev's original intention, but things did not work out that way. The reason for this lies primarily in Insarov's rather unsatisfactory characterization. He is of much less interest than Elena because Turgenev proved less than successful at portraying such a fictional personality. Insarov emerges as more of a symbol of what Turgenev saw as a revolutionary rather than as a credible human being. His is certainly a less complicated personality than either Rudin's or Lavretsky's. True, Rudin seemed to have no core to his being, and the same may be said of Insarov. With Rudin this was an intentional flaw of character that Turgenev saw as central to such people, but with Insarov it is a flaw in Turgenev's conception. Insarov is so one-dimensional that the reader's attention is drawn, almost perforce, to Elena. She is portrayed with such depth and intensity, her multifaceted personality is illuminated so brightly, that the central position in the novel becomes hers. The centrality of his heroine is something new for Turgenev: where Natalya had served more to enlighten the reader about Rudin, and Liza, to a lesser extent, about Lavretsky, here Insarov tells us more about Elena.

Turgenev's methods of characterization also shift in *On the Eve*. Elena's personality is revealed, not only through her relationship with Insarov and direct authorial description, but also through the comments and actions of the minor characters, especially Bersenev and more particularly Shubin, whose artist's eye sees much within her that others miss, and he also reveals the contrasting sides of Insarov's personality in two sculptures he makes of him. Turgenev also introduces rather more subjective information here than he does in his first two novels—letter, diary, dream—to delineate the thoughts and emotions of his characters, especially in relation to Elena. The resulting portrait of her verges on the sentimental in places, and Elena herself certainly lacks the intellectual interests of Rudin or Lavretsky, but there is no doubt that she ranks as the most intriguing, convincing, and memorable of all of Turgenev's many heroines. The fact that she is also decisive, firm, and strong-willed, and not only speaks but acts in a way in which Turgenev would have wished his heroes to, makes her portrait the more striking. Yet her devotion to a cause, her willing self-sacrifice, and her complete disregard for all the physical and material deprivations these entail, unite her with Liza. She also shares Liza's religious conviction that in some way God will punish her for daring to be happy. Although Turgenev allows her love to continue far longer than that of any other of his heroines, at the end he is just as pessimistic about the possibilities of human happiness being achieved through love as ever.

Despite its central love story, *On the Eve* is plainly a novel of ideas. Set "on the eve" of the Crimean War, published "on the eve" of the Emancipation, the novel describes the younger and more radical elements emerging in Russian society in the 1850s in contrast to the older and more conservative ones Turgenev had portrayed in *Rudin* and *Home of the Gentry.* He made his hero a Bulgarian because he could discern no such revolutionary types in the Russian men of the period. The nearest thing to a Russian revolutionary is Elena, and yet despite this aspect of her she also raises the question of the subordinate position of women in Russian society and the issue of whether they should have a formal education. However, the younger Russians whom Turgenev depicts do not prove as "superfluous" as their predecessors. What Turgenev admired in the younger generation is quite clear: "It's a matter of youth, glory, courage," says Shubin, recalling Mikhalevich's remonstration to Lavretsky. "Death, life, struggle, defeat, victory, love, freedom, fatherland. . . . May God grant it to everyone." He continues in that vein as he likens the older generation to people sitting in a swamp trying to give the impression that everything is a matter of indifference to them when for the younger generation "it's the whole world, or nothing!" But as yet they lack leaders, there are only "small fry . . . carniverous parasites . . . boasters and windbags," or introspective nonentities engrossed in their own paltry feelings. "When will our time come?" he cries. "When will real people arise amongst us?" In Shubin's opinion, Elena, that "sensitive spirit," would not have forsaken family and country if she had found a real man in Russia, and the reader senses that this is Turgenev's opinion too. The whole of Russian society is that swamp with its restrictive conventions, its patriarchal organization, its economic, intellectual, and spiritual poverty. If things are left to the older generation with its limited vision, then Russia will never change substantially. For the first time in his fiction Turgenev suggests that it is not people of his own class who will show the way, but the newer, poorer, gentry and *raznochintsy*, or people from classes other than the gentry, people like Bersenev, Shubin, even Insarov, and especially Elena, who deserts her gentry upbringing and its traditions by uniting herself with Insarov. In this sense *On the Eve* is far more optimistic about the future than anything Turgenev had written before.

The unison of new ideas, the adoption of those which do not divide people from one another but rather unite them, the importance of art, freedom, science, justice, and in particular the conception of love not as selfish eroticism but as sacrifice, all these ideas combined with that of national liberation inspired the critic Nikolay Dobrolyubov to compose his hostile but very influential critique of the novel entitled "Kogda zhe pridet nastoyashchy den'?" ("When will the real day come?"). For Dobrolyubov Elena foreshadows the appearance of a Russian Insarov. The ideal of national liberation implies the ridding of Russia not of foreign domination, which is Insarov's cause, but of the enemy within: not the Turks but "the damp and foggy atmosphere of our lives"—or in other, uncensored words, autocracy itself, and the social and economic systems that supported it. Dobrolyubov thought the time had indeed arrived for the "new people" to appear; Russia could not forever be "on the eve." He attacked the reformers of Russian society while appearing to fulminate against the "superfluous man" embodied in Turgenev's heroes. The reason why "new men" were so urgently needed, he said, is that the Russian literary hero usually came from the educated, wealthy segment of society and was consequently tied by blood and tradition to the very thing against which he should be rebelling (although we might note that most later Russian revolutionaries, including the Bolsheviks, came from the ranks of the landed gentry.) Turgenev read Dobrolyubov's review in proof and begged the editor of *Contemporary* not to publish it. "It can cause me nothing but unpleasantness," he wrote to Nekrasov on 19 February 1860. "It is unjust and sharp." Probably what annoyed Turgenev the most was the political message that Dobrolyubov extracted from the novel and which Turgenev himself had not intended.

Nor was Dobrolyubov the only one to react adversely to the novel. Turgenev's friend Countess Lambert, perhaps the prototype for Liza in *Home of the Gentry*, dissuaded Turgenev from dedicating *On the Eve* to her because she thought Elena a "forward hussy" lacking in all femininity. Tolstoy found the work banal and suggested that sad men who did not know what they wanted in life should not write novels. In general terms the negative criticism concentrated either on the unsatisfactory characterization of Insarov or on what was considered Elena's outrageously immoral behavior. This latter criticism was fiercely attacked by the contemporary women's movement, even though Turgenev was as shocked by this interpretation as he had been by Dobrolyubov's. On the other hand, many others defended Turgenev, arguing that the poetic detail, and author's skill in composition, his apposite language, and the psychological accuracy of his portrayal of the heroine as well as a host of minor characters amply compensated for the lack of any profound thought in the book. The critic Apollon Grigorev held that Turgenev's only purpose in writing the novel, one he had attained, had been faithfully to represent two passionate people whose paths had crossed in a tragic and fateful way. The majority of contemporary commentators agreed that Turgenev had solved the literary and psychological problems he had faced (despite the obvious difficulties they all had with Insarov), but that he had been noticeably less successful in his treatment of the social and political questions at the forefront of the work.

If Turgenev was displeased with his readers' criticisms of *On the Eve* (he was always oversensitive to the public response to his writings anyway) he was to react with even more incomprehension, anger, self-justification, and depression to the reception of his next, and probably best, novel, *Fathers and Sons*, where he did attempt to portray the "new man" whose appearance in literature Dobrolyubov had awaited.

"Hamlet and Don Quixote"

In the same month that saw the appearance of *On the Eve* Turgenev published his essay "Hamlet and Don Quixote" in *Contemporary*. The essay was a lecture first delivered in St. Petersburg on 10 January 1860 and set forth ideas that had been maturing for some years. The earliest reference to them appears in a letter to Pauline Viardot of 25 December 1847, in which he muses on the hero of Calderón's *La vida es sueño* (*Life's a Dream*). Sigismond, he writes, is a Spanish Hamlet who exhibits the differences between the personalities of a northern European and a southern one. "I Iam let is more reflective, more subtle, more of the philosopher . . .," he wrote, "[but] he cannot do anything because of indecision, doubt, and intellectualizing." On the other hand, the Quixote type was probably presented to him forcibly in 1848 when he personally observed the revolutionaries in Paris, noting their fiery enthusiasm and its consequences. He discussed the contrast with his friends in the 1850s, and even Tolstoy approved of his general line of argument. Although those present at the first complete presentation of the finished lecture gave it an oversimplified interpretation— that Quixote represented the radicals of the time and Hamlet the superfluous men of the preceding two decades (after all Turgenev himself wrote that the Hamlets of this world are of no use to the masses)—this is still arguably the single work of Turgenev's with the clearest exposition of his view of the human personality.

Hamlet and Don Quixote represent for Turgenev two basic human types, although rarely is anyone clearly the one or the other. The Quixote type believes in truth and in the existence of something beyond the self. He is devoted to an ideal for which he will sacrifice everything. Even though that ideal may not necessarily be based on reality—people consider Quixote on occasion to be a madman—this neither deters him in any way nor lessens his sincerity. He is completely without egoism, even though he is slow to feel compassion and finds it difficult to concentrate on more than one thing at a time. He is free to change his opinions at will and is not greatly concerned that the reasons for the change might not be very logical: when he discovers his beloved is far different from what he imagined he simply blames everything on the magicians. The Quixotes are in some ways conservative; they generally respect the political and social status quo and their country's rulers and religion. They nonetheless regard themselves as free and respect the freedom of others. Whatever obstacles they may encounter, they never doubt their ultimate success. They may be slightly comic, but they represent progress for mankind.

By contrast, the Hamlets are concerned only with the self, in which they have little or no faith, and with the predicament in which they find themselves. Hamlet doubts everything, including himself, and punishes himself for it. He delights in studying his own faults without pity. Unlike Quixote, who can inspire love and laughter in others, Hamlet can inspire neither except in rather remarkable characters like Horatio. Nor can he behave decisively. He continually prevaricates—and kills Polonius by accident. Quixote tilts at windmills thinking they are giants, and prevents a boy from being physically punished, but he acts on impulse, never worrying about the consequences of his actions. Hamlet can never behave in this way. In preparing to sacrifice himself, he thinks first, he calculates and weighs all the consequences, he asks whether his actions will be useful. Consequently, he is scarcely capable of self-sacrifice. Hamlet's mood is one of melancholy and pessimism. He longs to experience strong emotion but his egotism and self-contempt prevent it. He looks on everything, himself included, with irony, but that does not cause him to feel Byronic contempt for the world at large: he is too concerned with his self for that. Quixote might feel hurt at the way the world treats him, but the only hurt felt by Hamlet is that which he inflicts upon himself. While we may laugh at Quixote for his illusions, who, Turgenev asks, can infallibly distinguish illusion from reality? What matters most is sincerity, will, and strength of conviction.

At the end of the lecture Turgenev tried to unite his two contrasting characters. Both their deaths have a certain nobility. Both Hamlet and Don Quixote are humble and submissive, the qualities Turgenev most admired in the Russian peasant, and their deaths express kindness and goodness. All else may be ephemeral, but love remains. The moral, if there is one, is that whatever Quixote has done and whatever Hamlet has not, the two are redeemed by kindness, goodness, and love. In many of his stories and novels Turgenev, himself a Hamlet, criticized the Hamlets and praised the Quixotes, the type he himself would have preferred to have been.

Rather surprisingly, Tolstoy justified Turgenev's life and works as follows in a letter written on 10 January 1884, nearly a quarter of a century after the first appearance of "Hamlet and Don Quixote." Tugenev, he said, "lived, sought for, and expressed in his works that which he found. . . . I think that there are three phases in his life and in his writings 1) Faith in beauty (a woman's love—art). . . . 2) Doubts about this and doubts about everything. . . . 3) A faith that was not formulated . . . but a faith in goodness, love, and self-sacrifice . . . that is expressed by all his heroes who sacrifice themselves, and most vividly of all and most charmingly in his 'Don Quixote' where the paradoxical quality and the special form freed him from feeling ashamed of his role as a preacher of the good."

Chapter Five
Fathers and Sons

Introduction

Although Turgenev never cared about participating actively in the political life of his country, and spent most of his adult life abroad anyway, a reading of his novels and correspondence shows that he always took a keen interest in what was taking place in his native country, the ideas being formulated there about Russia and its ultimate destiny, and the social and political events that came to his notice. His novels give the clearest picture that any nineteenth-century Russian writer has bequeathed to later generations of the social development of the not very numerous liberal, and later radical, elements within Russian society and the opposition they aroused. His writings are frequently concerned with the social, political, or moral arguments that raged in educated Russian society: the controversies between the Slavophile nationalists and those who looked to Western Europe for salvation, between the older conservatives and the younger liberals, then between these liberals and the radicals and, later, among the Populists of the 1870s. He was constantly aware that his readers looked to writers like him for guidance on all these matters and even for answers to Russia's many problems. But he did not pursue objectives of this sort. He never gave answers. He never preached, but described. He wished to understand what was happening and to explain it. He stood to one side, hoping to reproduce what he saw as objectively as he could. Politically he remained uncommitted, although he hated Russia's autocratic system and bemoaned as much as anyone the injustice, intolerance, backwardness, oppression, and inertia that prevailed in that country. He provided no answers to Russia's "accursed questions," upon which Russian writers were expected to pontificate. This continually infuriated his contemporaries, who accused him, and not without justification, of vacillation, of lacking firm ideals, opinions, or principles and of being a weak character afraid to take sides—like most of the heroes of his fiction. His arguments with Bakunin, Herzen, Chernyshevsky, and Dobrolyubov over Russia's destiny are all symptomatic of this. Yet he was not to be deterred. That was his way, and he would proceed as best he could. Although in his fourth published novel, *Fathers and Sons*, he still offers no conclusions, let alone the panaceas some demanded, it remains the most political of all his six novels.

When the long-awaited emancipation of the peasants was enacted on 19 February 1861, Annenkov sent Turgenev, who was in Paris at the time, a telegram with the news. The excitement felt by Turgenev and the few other liberal émigrés there was intense though short-lived. He and his friends immediately organized a dinner in honor of the czar, and there was a service of thanksgiving in the Russian Orthodox church in Paris. It soon became clear, however, that the peasants had not truly been freed; they remained serfs in all but name. The land they were allotted was either of poor quality or else insufficient to support them and their families; where this was not the case an excessively heavy financial burden was placed upon them in the form of long-term redemption payments. The radicals looked upon the emancipation quite simply as a fraud upon the peasantry, as a betrayal of their interests. The peasants themselves distrusted its confusing terms, refused on a large scale to accept them, and still hoped to receive the land as a gift. They soon expressed their distrust of the authorities, first in passive resistance and then with violent opposition. In July 1861 the "Land and Liberty" terrorist organization was set up, the first revolutionary group in Russia since the Decembrists of 1825. Various revolutionary pamphlets and manifestoes were secretly published and widely distributed, and consequently leading radicals and agitators were arrested, imprisoned, and exiled. Fires broke out in St. Petersburg, and university students were suspected of starting them. There was widespread unrest all over European Russia, and police activity intensified. In 1862 *Contemporary* was closed for eight months, Chernyshevsky was arrested in July, and the police began a long investigation (in which Turgenev was later involved) into possible connections between the revolutionaries inside Russia and leading exiles abroad, notably Herzen and Ogarev in London. The Russian authorities believed these two were the key to solving the problem of the disorders they were facing. Although this was not the case, there is no doubt that the influence of their journal *The Bell* inside Russia was enormous. The situation was further worsened by the government's refusal to weaken in any way the autocratic system of rule, which only proved to the radicals that support for the czar and his purportedly liberal reforms was out of the question.

While Turgenev sympathized with some of the radicals' ideas, although never with their revolutionary objectives, he abhorred their violent behavior. "The news from Russia distresses me," he wrote to Countess Lambert from Paris on 10 December 1861, when the situation was at its most worrying. "It is impossible for me in some respects not to blame my friends, but equally I cannot exonerate the government either." In his view violence, from which-ever side, could offer no solutions. Yet he was constantly aware that some-thing new was happening inside Russia, something he felt in the air everywhere but which he failed even to grasp, let alone comprehend. He was, however, fascinated by it and wished to investigate these "new people" and their ideas. Very different from men like himself, they had one important ad-vantage in his eyes: they were free from the romantic idealism that had dog-ged his own generation, and for better or worse he perceived that the future of his country lay in their hands. They might be wrong in some of their beliefs and in most of their methods, but they were determined to change things, something of which his own generation had been incapable. They might be-have in an uncivilized manner, but their enemies were his enemies too. They might heap acrimony on ineffectual liberals like him, but they wanted to rid Russia of despotism. For the rest of his novelistic life Turgenev attempted to understand them and to explain them, with *Fathers and Sons* as his first ef-fort, even though he later claimed that he started with no preconceptions or even any clear idea of the direction the novel would take. "Don't laugh," he later wrote to Mikhail Saltykov-Shchedrin on 15 January 1876, "but there was something stronger than the author himself, something independent of him. I wrote . . . as if I was amazed myself at what was emerging." Yet what he wrote was no political pamphlet (that was unfortunately to come). He views all the arguments he discusses and attempts to analyze as differences in human personality and temperament, and it is through these that ideological conflicts are expressed.

Such, briefly, is the background against which *Fathers and Sons* was planned, written, and read. The first mention of the novel occurs in a letter he wrote to Countess Lambert on 6 August 1860, while he was on holiday in Ventnor on the Isle of Wight. His outline of the book had been worked out by the end of the following month, and he had finished the first half or so of the manuscript by the end of the winter, while he was living in Paris. He re-turned to Spasskoe in the spring of 1861 and had completed the first draft by mid-summer. As usual, he submitted it to his friends for their comments and criticisms, and made many consequent changes. Annenkov raised two inter-esting points. One concerned the arguments between radical and conserva-tive in which the latter stresses that "it is civilization which is dear to us" to the contemptuous scorn of the former. This reflects a major difference between the old landowning gentry and the rising class from the masses, with their lack of respect for all vestiges of the past. Annenkov also noticed the elitism of the radicals of the 1860s, noticeably absent from the populists of the 1870s, whose general humility before what they considered the wisdom of the peasantry Turgenev described in his last novel, *Virgin Soil*. Turgenev readily incorporated both of Annenkov's suggestions into the novel. Turgenev finally gave the completed manuscript to Katkov in August 1861. Although Katkov still saw it as a panegyric to the revolutionaries, "the apotheosis of *Contemporary*," as he rather stupidly described it, and wanted Turgenev to soften some of his descriptions, the novel appeared early in 1862 in his *Russian Herald*.

Story and Construction

Like all but the last of Turgenev's novels, *Fathers and Sons* has a straightforward story line. Its time scale is short: from 20 May 1859 to that August, with a few words at the end describing the lives of some of the characters up until the following January. Its twenty-eight chapters begin with the arrival of two university students, Arkady Kirsanov and Evgeny Bazarov, to stay at Marino, the country home of Arkady's widowed father, Nikolay Petrovich, an affectionate and kindly man whose small estate is in poor condition and badly run. After the death of his wife Nikolay had grown fond of a peasant girl, Fenichka, and taken her into his home, where she has borne him a son. The other member of the household is Nikolay's brother Pavel, an Anglophile dandy whose life has been empty since an unhappy love affair in his youth and who has made of himself a foppish, irritable, and intolerant recluse. Turgenev clearly intended Bazarov, a medical student, to represent the "new men and women" who were becoming the idols of the younger generation of the intelligentsia. In their own words, Bazarov and his "disciple" Arkady are nihilists, which means, as they define it, that they accept absolutely nothing on trust and put everything to the test of pragmatic reason. Much of the novel's dialogue is concerned with the exposition of Bazarov's ideas. The first third of the book details the differences in social background, upbringing, and opinion between Bazarov (and consequently of the "new people" in general) and the older Kirsanov brothers, especially Pavel. Turgenev saw all their divergences as stemming from a difference in age, and hence the novel's title. The mutual antagonism and incomprehension apparent from the outset in the attitudes of Bazarov and Pavel culminates in a duel, the outcome of which is inconclusive both physically and metaphorically.

The second section of *Fathers and Sons* deals with the moral of the story, if such a word may be used in this connection. In Turgenev's view the extreme radical views expressed by Bazarov engender another conflict, that between ideas and human nature, indeed Nature itself, and human nature is ultimately triumphant. Turgenev illustrates this theme in two main ways. First,

he has Bazarov fall in love with a well-off, cold young widow, Anna
Sergeevna Odintsova, despite his rejection of romantic love and his protestations that the relations between the sexes are strictly physical. Odintsova ultimately rejects his love, but he finds for the first time in his life that he is in
love with a woman and that he cannot suppress this love. Second, human nature also prevails in the case of Arkady, who over the summer finds himself
attracted to Odintsova's younger sister Katya. In his final parting from
Bazarov Arkady realizes that all his own professed views on nihilism were
mere infatuation, and that what he really wanted and always had wanted
from life were love and marriage.

The final third of the book deals largely with Bazarov's return to his own
family, his painful relationship with his simple-hearted, lovable, and slightly
comic old parents, who dote on him, and his death from typhus following an
autopsy on a peasant. The novel ends with one of the most moving passages
Turgenev ever wrote, describing Bazarov's parents crying and praying at the
graveside of their only son. "Can it be," asks Turgenev, "that their prayers and
tears are fruitless? Oh, no! Whatever the passionate, sinful, and rebellious
heart that has been covered by the grave, the flowers that grow on it look
upon us serenely with their innocent eyes. They do not speak to us only of
eternal peace, of that great peace of 'indifferent' nature: they speak also of
eternal reconciliation and of life everlasting." Nature might be indifferent,
but human beings are still powerless before it. And the final words of the passage strike a religious note rare in Turgenev.

Although hardly as well constructed, as one critic has suggested,[1] as a play
by Sophocles, *Fathers and Sons* does display a certain inevitability, an inner
logic of progression, and all its various parts do form a cohesive whole. It contains both the tragic and the comic in the classical sense, at least as understood
in certain modern interpretations of Aristotle's *Poetics*, and these contrasting
elements are very satisfactorily integrated. It is tragic in the sense that the hero
is excluded from a certain society by differing from it and remains in isola-
tion, that he bears within himself the seeds of his own downfall, that he is de-
ceived about his own personality, especially his positive qualities, and that he
finally comes to a realization of the truth before his death. All of this clearly
applies to Bazarov. It is comic in dealing with integration into a given society.
Usually, in this interpretation, the "hero" and "heroine" are not particularly
remarkable personalities, although possessed of positive qualities of character. In *Fathers and Sons* this would apply to Arkady and Katya and to Nikolay
and Fenichka. The progress of such pairs toward happiness is normally hin-
dered by other, and markedly more interesting, characters who are removed
at the end either by joining the society or by leaving it altogether. This theory

may easily be applied to *Fathers and Sons*, with its two sets of "heroes and heroines." On the one hand there are Arkady and Katya, and on the other Nikolay and Fenichka, whose journey toward happiness—here equated with marriage—is thwarted by Bazarov and Pavel, respectively. Both of these are removed at the end, one by death, the other by emigration. It could also be argued that both Bazarov and Pavel before their respective ends do achieve an intergration of sorts with society inasmuch as both of them give approval to the marriages they had earlier opposed. Bazarov does it in a negative way by abandoning his friendship with Arkady and leaving him to his fate, and Pavel positively by pleading with Nikolay to marry Fenichka and thus regularize their position.

David Lowe has convincingly argued that *Fathers and Sons* may be seen as a series of interlocking journeys during which there occurs a series of confrontations.[2] The journeys take the reader from the Kirsanov estate in Marino to town, from town to the Odintsova estate at Nikolskoe, from Nikolskoe to Bazarov's parental home, and from there, via separate visits, to Nikolskoe and then back to Marino. In these varied settings the main characters find themselves in different circumstances and react accordingly. At Marino Arkady is in a familiar environment while Bazarov is the stranger; at Bazarov's parents' home the situation is reversed, however much and pointedly it is Arkady who feels the more at home, while at Nikolskoe both Arkady and Bazarov are strangers while Odintsova and Katya are on home territory. We also see both Arkady and Bazarov individually at Nikolskoe on different occasions: Arkady feels at ease, and Bazarov quite the reverse. All through these various visits we get the clear impression that Arkady is the more relaxed in a traditional environment, while Bazarov remains the eternal stranger. Finally, we see Arkady and Bazarov at their respective parental homes, without the company of the other.

During these journeys, or visits, the major confrontations of the novel occur: those between Bazarov and the Kirsanov brothers, between Arkady and his father, between Bazarov and Odintsova, and between Bazarov and his parents. The confrontations are on the one hand social and political, and on the other emotional. The arguments betwen Bazarov and Pavel in particular reflect the ideological conflict in the Russia of the 1860s, the outcome of which is as inconclusive as the duel the two fight. The emotional differences are most clearly depicted in the relationship between Bazarov and Odintsova, which is resolved, but also in those among Bazarov and Arkady and Nikolay. The ideological disputes remain largely unresolved, which is only to be expected from Turgenev, while the emotional conflicts are all settled— unhappily for Bazarov and Pavel, neutrally for Odintsova, and (rare in

Turgenev) happily for both Nikolay and Fenichka and for Arkady and
Katya.

Characters and Themes

By the time *Fathers and Sons* was written Turgenev's methods of characterization were well established. The reader learns the appropriate details of
each character from three different sources: direct authorial description, the
characters' own words about themselves, and what other characters say about
them. Consequently, dialogue is a frequent device for imparting this information, as are also the pauses or silences within it. Usually the more important Turgenev thinks a character, the more details about him he provides:
physical appearance, habits of dress and speech, prehistory. He also includes
a form of epilogue describing some of his characters' lives (although in *Fathers and Sons* it is very brief, almost apologetic). Although Turgenev takes
great pains to tell his reader what his characters are thinking and feeling, he
rarely expounds on their psychological motivations, being content to concentrate on surface phenomena. He was incapable of the sort of detailed psychological analysis in which Tolstoy indulged, and was even distrustful of it. He
had very set opinions about the limits of depiction. A sensitive reader, he was
convinced, will understand with a minimum of explanation; too much information merely leads to boredom. A few observations should suffice to demonstrate this. He replaces such detail with contrast and juxtaposition, with
description rather than analysis. Nor are many of his characters sharply indi-
vidualized; they tend rather to be representative of a group as well as themselves. All human beings, Turgenev suggests, have certain characteristics in
common, and consequently there is a limit to the number of possible reactions to a given situation. A particular type of personality will react in a certain way. This would support the suggestion that most of Turgenev's
characters can be viewed in pairs, or in groups. These pairings are often of
likes, but sometimes of unlikes. The similarities of each individual within the
pair tell as much about the other member as do the dissimilarities.

Such established methods of characterization are used in *Fathers and Sons*.
There are, however, some innovations too, and it is perhaps they, and the differences from his other novels, that make *Fathers and Sons* the best and most
distinctive of his novels. In other words, *Fathers and Sons* is somewhat atypi-
cal. It may be his most successful book because Turgenev at last dealt with
the problem that had long concerned him, and which he would never solve
any more satisfactorily: the task of integrating the imaginative theme of the
love story with the social observations he wished to make. So well does he

fuse the two elements that it is possible today to read the novel without being at all concerned about the ideological conflicts of the 1860s with which Turgenev was very much involved. Other ideas are also successfully integrated in the book: the notion that children are very like their fathers, the importance of family and home, the proposition that man's endeavors and achievements are largely transient, that only life and its true, eternal values are important. All these ideas and themes are expressed through the characters Turgenev so skillfully presents.

There can be no doubt, however, that Turgenev wished primarily to analyze the arguments among members of the Russian intelligentsia at the end of the 1850s and the start of the 1860s. The root of the conflict lay, in his opinion, in the differences between the generations of the 1840s and the 1860s. The earlier generation was of the gentry class, drew its ideas from German romantic philosophy and English liberalism, and favored reforms, though gradual ones instituted from above. On the other hand, the generation of the 1860s sprang from the *raznochintsy*, who placed their faith in the natural sciences and materialism. With no respect for traditions and no belief in reform, they favored fundamental change, and revolution if necessary. Turgenev transmutes this conflict through his characters, on the one hand Nikolay and Pavel Kirsanov as representatives of the older generation and, on the other, Bazarov and at the start Arkady as typical of the younger. The differences between them are apparent from the beginning, and the novel's major confrontations occur between Pavel and Bazarov.

In an unusual step, Turgenev introduces his main hero at the outset, before even establishing the "place" firmly. Bazarov is brought home by Arkady to visit after the two have graduated from university. Bazarov is curt, abrupt, off-hand. He and Pavel take an immediate dislike to each other; each sees in the other all he despises in other people. Detailed differences in upbringing, social class, attitudes, and personality soon emerge. By the novel's conclusion, however, the two have at least reached a certain understanding of each other, even though they remain mutually antipathetic. An anglophile, Pavel is in his mid-forties. He is vain. He is fastidious about his dress and his toilette. He is proud and stubborn, opinionated and absorbed in himself. He has no appreciation of nature, he reads rarely, and displays little interest in the arts in general despite his belief in their value. His speech is idiosyncratic, overcorrect, and a little affected, just like his clothes and the furnishings in his rooms. Such a manner gives his life a stability he craves after the experiences of his youth.

As a young man Pavel was brought up at home and then enrolled in the Corps of Pages. He led the typical life of the well-off, carefree, young nobleman. Remarkably good-looking and self-confident, he had a biting sense of humor. Once commissioned as an officer, he became the dashing man-about-town who gave himself airs that only added to his attractiveness. Immensely charming, he found that men thought him a fop but secretly envied him while women lost their heads over him—a situation of which he took every advantage while remaining emotionally uninvolved. An apparently brilliant career lay ahead of him when suddenly everything changed. He met a certain Princess R., an eccentric, frivolous woman who gave herself over to every pleasure. But at night she would cry and pray and find no peace. Though not unduly attractive, she had a good figure and wonderfully penetrating eyes. Accustomed to easy conquests, Pavel soon succeeded with her too. Tormented even when his attentions were reciprocated, he hardly knew what to do when he found himself for the first time in his life actually in love and all too soon rejected. He followed the princess abroad and spent four years pursuing her. Finally he returned to Russia, wandered from place to place, and made a few more meaningless conquests, but as he aged he grew bitterly disenchanted. Ten drab years later, in 1848, he learned of the death of the princess and then settled with his brother on his country estate. At the novel's opening he is a lonely bachelor who has entered upon "that indefinite, twilight period of regrets that are akin to hopes . . . when youth is over and old age has not yet come."

Of Bazarov's prehistory, by contrast, Turgenev tells us very little. This is another unusual facet of his characterization, one partly explained by Turgenev's own lack of knowledge about the origins of the sort of people he wished to portray through Bazarov, so that he had to describe him as he was. But this method also makes him more mysterious: in some ways he remains as enigmatic to the reader as did Princess R. to Pavel.

When Bazarov first arrives at Marino Pavel finds him "uncivil." Arkady attempts to excuse his friend by saying that this is only his manner, and that he cannot stand ceremony. He later explains that Bazarov is a "nihilist," a term neither Pavel nor Nikolay understands. Nikolay suggests it might denote a man who recognizes nothing, to which Arkady responds that a nihilist "doesn't take any principle for granted, however much that principle is revered." Pavel is horrified. Without principles, he says, his generation "couldn't move an inch or draw a single breath." The stage is immediately set for the major verbal confrontation between Pavel and Bazarov.

On the day after his arrival at Marino Bazarov returns from collecting frogs which he plans to dissect. Pavel, spoiling for a fight, questions Bazarov, who declares that his only interests lie in physics and the natural sciences. An argument rapidly develops. Bazarov also seems indifferent to Pavel, and this irritates Pavel because he cannot accept the notion that "this son of an army doctor" can be so self-assured in his presence, so churlish and insolent. Pavel interrogates Bazarov on his beliefs: Does he accept nothing on trust? Does he accept no authority? "What am I to believe?" Bazarov objects. "If people talk sense then I agree with them. That's all there is to it." Pavel retorts that the Germans who produced Goethe and Schiller now put forth only chemists, to which Bazarov replies that "a decent chemist is twenty times more useful than any poet." Their mutual antagonism, born of both social and temperamental causes, increases. Later on Arkady accuses Bazarov of not wishing to understand his uncle, or of not realizing that his education is partly responsible for his character. Bazarov suggests that with proper education all Pavel's ills, and indeed all of Russia's, will disappear. He refuses to soften even when Arkady recounts the story of Pavel and Princess R.: "I must say that a fellow who stakes his whole life on the card of a woman's love and when that card fails turns bitter and becomes fit for nothing is no man." There are no mysterious relations between a man and a woman. If you study the anatomy of the eye, what is the source of an enigmatic look? "That's all romantic nonsense, rotten aesthetics," he declares. But Bazarov is soon forced to put his views on love to the test.

In the meantime, a fortnight passes at Marino during which everything continues as before. Through a series of conversations, arguments, and altercations Turgenev reveals more of Bazarov's character. His character traits include dedication to hard work, an aggressive materialism, a rejection of imaginative literature (Bazarov urges Nikolay to cease reading Pushkin and gives him Ludwig Büchner's materialistic *Kraft und Stoff* instead), an ability to get along with the peasants even though he tends to laugh at them and their ways, and a conviction that men like Nikolay might well be good men but they are now out of date. Bazarov is highly intelligent, knowledgeable, and articulate when forced to be. He recognizes no principles; what is valuable and must be retained is only the useful. The most useful thing for him to do is to negate and to question everything: art, poetry, civilization, social structures, traditional values and modes of thought and behavior, everything. Talking is of no more use in helping Russia; what is needed now is action, and destructive action at that. Bazarov feels no need to suggest anything to replace that which has been destroyed. He fights for no "cause" in that respect. All Bazarov's opinions and attitudes are eagerly supported by Arkady, fiercely refuted by Pavel, and treated rather resignedly by Nikolay.

Up until this point Bazarov might have emerged as one-dimensional as had Insarov before him. Turgenev has described much of what Bazarov thinks and how he behaves, but has offered us little about his personality save for characteristics that he thinks typical of his generation rather than the individual. The second two thirds of the novel delineate a different and far more revealing side to his nature. Here too Turgenev fully integrates the characters he creates and the story he wishes to tell about them with the social background and problems he felt obliged to discuss. Bazarov's relationship with Odintsova reflects not only their differing personalities but also their different social classes and the attitudes linked to them. Again we have the problem of the men of the 1840s and the 1860s, the gentry versus the *raznochintsy*. This question is reflected in parallel love stories that Turgenev interweaves throughout the novel: Nikolay and his wife, Nikolay and Fenichka, Arkady and Odintsova, Arkady and Katya, Pavel and Princess R. Even what passes between Bazarov and Fenichka, Pavel's feelings for Fenichka and her attitude to him have the same purpose: to reveal character and social background. They represent personality as well as ideology. This may hardly be said of Lavretsky and Liza or of Insarov and Elena, neither of whose relationships has much to do with the social and political problems of their day, although it could be argued that Rudin's inability to respond to Natalya's love reflects his generation's inability to act on any level.

Odintsova is one of Turgenev's most interesting heroines and apparently one of the most complex. He described her elsewhere as a representative of "our idle, dreaming, curious, and cold, epicurean gentry ladies." All that she certainly is. She is introduced to Bazarov and Arkady at a ball in the provincial capital, and Turgenev initially describes her through her effect on Arkady. She is twenty-nine, tall, dignified, and graceful, with tranquil and intelligent eyes. A gentle strength radiates from her face. She is far from loquacious, but everything she says strikes Arkady as showing that she has experienced and pondered much. She bewitches Arkady, who is horrified when Bazarov adopts a merely physical attitude toward her: he admires her shoulders and wonders "what sort of a mammal she is." He tells Arkady that the only point in chasing after a woman is to achieve your goal. If you do, well and good, and that's an end of it; if you don't, forget her. There are plenty more women around.

In chapter 15 Turgenev gives a different view of Odintsova through authorial description which helps to fit her into her class, background, and times. The daughter of a nobleman who had ruined himself at cards and then died, the twenty-year-old Odintsova was left with her younger sister Katya to lead a lonely, impecunious country life. She met a wealthy hypochondriac whose proposal she accepted, thereby causing much malicious gossip. Some six years later he died, bequeathing her a luxurious house that she rarely left. Aloof in manner, independent and self-contained in character, she lived in a calm seldom disturbed, and then only briefly. She had a need for stability and order. "You cannot live in the country without order," she tells Bazarov when he remarks on her punctuality and set patterns of behavior. "Otherwise you'd die of boredom." She was as tranquil spiritually as she was in her daily life. She slept motionlessly, "all pure and frigid in her clean and fragrant linen." Like Pavel, she is largely indifferent to the arts and to nature. Like him too, she possesses strength of will which in her case proves greater than even Bazarov's. Her emotions occasionally seem a little contradictory when sometimes it appears that she does not know what she wants. She strikes others, and especially men, as a passionate woman, but she is not. She keeps her emotions normally under as much control as her life in general, but ultimately they are dead. Initially Bazarov poses a physical and emotional threat to her ordered life, and she rejects his love because she cannot broach any upset. What might have been between her and Bazarov only momentarily crosses her mind. He might terrify her but she will not allow him to affect her life. She takes refuge in Arkady's adoration. She admits to being quite fond of Arkady, yet realizes that he can never be more than "the boy" as opposed to "the wolf," Bazarov. Her marriage at the end of the novel to a considerate, up-and-coming lawyer is typical of her. She takes—not for love but for convenience and out of conviction—a husband as emotionally cold as she is. She will not compromise her desire for personal freedom unencumbered by emotional complications, as Bazarov discovers to his cost. His brief acquaintance with her is the catalyst for a further stage in his journey toward self-knowledge.

Turgenev is content to demonstrate Bazarov's strength of character through his effect on others. All the other characters in the novel react strongly to him. Arkady adopts his opinions and tries to model himself on him, Pavel is irritated by him and grows to despise and hate him, Nikolay is fascinated by him yet mistrusts him, Sitnikov—a young poseur who spouts nihilist and other views—cowers before him, the peasants at first take to him but later reject him, Katya sees him as a wild beast, Odintsova is excited and frightened by him, Fenichka is enchanted by him, and his parents dote upon him. His vulnerability, however, is shown rather more from within than from without. Always seeking to live up to his convictions, he is prepared to take chances (unlike any of the other characters) to put them to the test, and to change them if they prove wrong. He does this with Odintsova by testing his view that love is all romantic nonsense. The result, though, surprises him. His feelings for her, and the passion that he experiences when he brutally kisses her, seem inexplicable to him. They are not subject to the practical or materialistic yardstick by which he measures everything. He finds he cannot take the advice he gave to Arkady when all three first met.

After his experience with Odintsova, Bazarov might appear to be a different man from the one Turgenev depicted before their fateful meeting. But he is not. Rather, he has found some of his convictions wanting, and for the first time in his life is at a loss. But his reaction is in no sense out of character. Nor is his retreat afterward to his parental home in any way surprising. Odintsova has revealed to him an aspect of his personality of which he had previously been unaware. He had denied the power of love (or even its existence) before he had encountered it, just as he had denied everything else. He then accepts his discovery, however unfortunate for him it may be. His empiricism lasts to the very end. So does his quest for self-awareness. His behavior does change for a time, but this is in reaction to what he has learned about himself from his relations with Odintsova. He becomes less solitary for a while. He flirts with Fenichka, something he would never have even contemplated before, and his kissing her is probably the only ignoble act of his life. It has, however, serious consequences. His impulsive action is seen by Pavel, who uses his clear affection for Fenichka, albeit more avuncular than anything else, and his respect for his brother as excuses to bring his differences with Bazarov to a head. He calls Bazarov out for a duel. Bazarov is both rather bemused and a little amused, but he does not decline. Normally a man of Pavel's class would have thought it beneath his dignity to fight someone like Bazarov: the prince in "The Diary of a Superfluous Man" had reacted in this way to Chulkaturin's challenge. But Pavel's intense dislike of Bazarov drives him to disregard convention. Even the terrified peasant who is compelled to witness the duel thinks it all wrong, "not at all the way the real gentry should behave." And Bazarov temporarily sets aside those convictions that should have prevented him from accepting such a confrontation. The outcome, though, is inconclusive. Pavel fires first and misses; Bazarov wounds Pavel in the leg; and both dispense with the customary right to a second shot. If the duel has any significance beyond that of a clash of two opposing personalities which tells each as much about himself as it does about the other, or that of suggesting the breakdown of the traditional class differences in Russia, or that Turgenev is making a metaphorical point about the rift between the men of the 1840s and those of the 1860s, then there is neither clear winner nor obvious loser; neither proves superior to the other. Bazarov turns out to be magnanimous however pointless he might think the duel in the first place: he tends Pavel's wounds. Pavel realizes he has made himself look silly, yet finds the strength, perhaps grudgingly, to forgive Bazarov some of their differences. In this way the duel can be interpreted as showing that although in Turgenev's view there can be only antagonism between the generations, there is at least some small hope that they can attain some mutual understanding.

After the duel Pavel recovers, urges Nikolay to marry Fenichka— something he had previously opposed—and leaves Russia to spend the rest of his lonely life in Dresden. Bazarov finds himself more and more irritated at Arkady who, he discovers, has really only played at being a nihilist and is just as hopeless in Bazarov's eyes as his father Nikolay. They argue and almost come to blows, but, as in the duel, Bazarov avoids the violence his views would justify. He returns home to his parents, starts providing medical aid to the local peasantry, and dies shortly afterward from typhus. It seems farfetched to suggest that Turgenev has given him some innate death wish, or that his death is a form of suicide following Odintsova's rejection of his love, even though Turgenev felt that men such as Bazarov were doomed because their time had not yet arrived. The only hint that could possibly support such an interpretation is the fact that Bazarov is pessimistic about the future of Russia at the start and pessimistic about his own place in it at the end. It is his nature to challenge, to repudiate, and to deny. Death is no exception, but death will not be thwarted. This rough-hewn, dedicated, and honest man with all his unused strength represents the power of human reason. But he is first defeated by a passion (love for a woman that he tries to suppress and deny as he does everything else), and then not by his own carelessness but by heartless nature, which Turgenev conceives of as a cold-eyed goddess who does not concern herself with good or evil, art or beauty. Still less are human beings of concern to her. They will not be saved by egoism or altruism, by faith, convictions, or actions. Nature is indifferent; her laws are her own. Tragically, Bazarov realizes this too late. Despite all the social questions Turgenev wished to treat and for all his intentions of making Bazarov something of a mystery, it is the human predicament that primarily interested him. Bazarov's political opinions are secondary. His futile death underscores the relative insignificance of his philosophy and the transience of social problems. For Turgenev ultimately the only things of lasting importance are not the particular but the more general—art, nature, love, the family, the positive sides of human behavior. He admires Bazarov for his strength of character, his integrity, his courage, and his pursuit of the truth, both about himself and about the world he lived in. That his opinions were wrong is a secondary matter.

We may adopt a similar approach to most of the other characters as well. Nikolay Kirsanov is a kindly, retiring individual. Normally a man of melancholy mood, he is rather timid and easily moved to tears. He tries to convince himself that he is progressive and keeps up with the times, and thus is extremely upset when Bazarov tells him that "his song is sung." Although he thinks the younger generation might be right on some points, he nonetheless believes that his beliefs are nearer the truth. However, he lacks heart for the struggle and reacts to change badly. Nikolay does not cope with life's difficulties at all well either. He seems to be dogged by bad luck. He broke his leg just before he was about to enlist in the army, his happy first marriage was cut short by his wife's sudden death, and his plans to go abroad were upset by the events of 1848. He looked forward eagerly to Arkady's return from university, and was correspondingly disappointed when the "nihilist" Bazarov dismissed him and his entire generation. He worries about what people, especially the young, think of him. He will not marry Fenichka until he obtains the approval of both Pavel and Arkady. He loves nature, music, and poetry. Turgenev presents him as typical of the kind-hearted but completely ineffectual gentry. Typically too, his estates are in a sorry state. His peasants do not pay their tithes, his trees do not flourish, his pond never fills up as it should, and his well produces only brackish water. These poor conditions strike Arkady forcibly on his return. "No," he thought, "there is no prosperity here, no sign of contentment or hard work. It just can't go on like this. It must all be transformed. . . . But how are we to do it? Where should we begin?" Arkady, like his father, is representative of his class: he can see his problems but can offer no solution to them. Yet despite his past misfortunes Nikolay ends up with a loving wife, a devoted son, and his home, however outwardly unprepossessing: he has his "nest." Turgenev continually suggests that this is a very positive feature of human existence in an ephemeral world. And it is a "nest" to which Arkady returns too; even Bazarov's return to his parents' can be seen as an attempt to recapture in the surroundings of his parental home the stability that his life has lost, and that he cannot find anywhere else.

Much to Turgenev's surprise, some of his younger readers paid less attention to the Kirsanov brothers or even Bazarov than to Arkady, whom they considered the most successfully drawn character in the whole novel. Despite his admiration for Bazarov and his imitation of his ideas, he very much resembles his father. Their lives follow similar patterns. Raised initially at home in provincial Russia, both are taken by their fathers to St. Petersburg to university. Both successfully graduate and return home. Both marry and run their estates, and Arkady's success will probably be no greater than Nikolay's. Arkady is also similar in character to his father. He has comparable likes and dislikes, at least once Bazarov's influence has been eliminated. He has as much liking for music, art, and poetry. He is as retiring and old-fashioned. There is nothing in any way outstanding about either of them; they are both average men of their generation and class. They might think their own thoughts and have their own opinions, but all in all they fit in with the time-honored traditions of thought and behavior expected of them.

Katya recognizes this instinctively. Not at all afraid of life, not at all bashful, she exhibits, like her elder sister, an independence of thought and behavior, but within prescribed limits. Very perspicacious, she understands other people well. Rather like Natasha Rostova in Tolstoy's *War and Peace*, she derives this understanding not from intelligence but from intuition. She realizes that Arkady is not the nihilist he purports to be. Once he is over his mild infatuation with Odintsova, and Bazarov has left, she falls in love with him and rapidly transforms him into the "domesticated animal" he is at heart. Their marriage will be much like Nikolay's, as Turgenev again stresses the importance of home and close family ties.

This emerges again with Bazarov's parents, Vasily and Arina. Whereas the generation gap is easily bridged by Arkady and his father because it does not really exist between them in the first place, it is sadder for the Bazarovs. Despite their constant, and indeed gently comic, attempts to understand and please their only son, Bazarov is rudely uncaring toward them. Vasily fears his son's reproval. He conceals from him the religious side of his nature and hides his military decorations. He is terrified when he learns that Bazarov knows he has had a peasant flogged. Like Nikolay, he likes to think he keeps abreast of recent developments, and is just as weak in the face of a strong personality. He is as typical of his class as Nikolay, and the differences between them are evident. Thus both like music, but the Kirsanovs play Mozart and Schubert while Vasily hums Meyerbeer. The Kirsanovs know French, German, and English, while Vasily with his *gymnazium* education knows only Latin and cannot speak to the German doctor, whom Odintsova brings to tend Bazarov, in his native tongue. The Kirsanovs are not in any way religious, while Vasily and Arina are: Arina has a profound and unquestioning faith and is very superstitious. They both lack the social graces that are part of the Kirsanovs' and the Odintsovas' way of life. Turgenev skillfully portrays not only the ideological differences between the generations as he sees them but also differences of personality and social standing. Speech, behavior, and thought patterns are all sharply delineated.

Critical Furor

When *Fathers and Sons* was published in early 1862 it created possibly the greatest controversy that has ever greeted a Russian novel, one centered almost entirely on the depiction of the novel's main protagonist, Bazarov. What was he? the readers and critics asked. What was Turgenev intending to

show through him? Was he a force for good or evil? Was he a hero or a villain?
All were agreed that he was young and enthusiastic about his beliefs, that he
was highly intelligent, and that he embodied hope for the future because he
had rejected the past. He was also far from the superfluous men of yesteryear
whom readers had come to expect from the pen of his creator. But was
Turgenev presenting a true portrait of the younger generation, or had he set
out to denigrate it?

We might recall that Turgenev himself was so engrossed in his creation
that he had kept a diary in Bazarov's name while writing the novel. In it he
noted his hero's reactions to social and political events of the day. Turgenev
then lent "this very substantial notebook" to a friend, who promptly mislaid
it. From a multitude of other sources, however, we know a great deal about
Turgenev's intentions. It is impossible to deny that he had the greatest sympathy for his hero. He was later to call Bazarov his "favorite offspring," and he
frequently spoke of his admiration for him. In this connection it should not
be forgotten that he dedicated the novel, when published as a book, to the
memory of Belinsky. Had he intended a negative portrait he would scarcely
have equated Bazarov with a man whom he venerated all his life. Yet the first
criticisms of the novel emerged from the ranks of the young radicals. They
could see nothing in the portrayal of Bazarov but a caricature (if caricatures
were needed, they should have paid more attention to Sitnikov and the ludi-
crous Kukshina): they viewed his portrayal as an attack upon themselves or
more particularly upon Chernyshevsky and Dobrolyubov. They were unrea-
sonable and hostile. Within a fortnight of the novel's original appearance in
the *Russian Herald* they came out in print. *Contemporary* published a vicious
and quite unwarranted attack upon Turgenev by Maksim Antonovich entitled "An Asmodeus of our Time" that even referred disparagingly to
Turgenev's relations with Pauline Viardot. In Jewish mythology Asmodeus is
always depicted as the evil demon who seeks to destroy young people's happiness by all sorts of calamities. Here Antonovich equated him with Bazarov,
vilifying Turgenev for his monstrous portrayal of the younger generation.
Bazarov, he wrote, was a sensualist whose only interests were in wine and
women. Despite his protestations to the contrary, Bazarov had no concern for
ordinary people at all. Turgenev, he said, despite his reputation in the past as
a champion of the underdog, had now patently joined the ranks of the dark-
est reactionaries.

Antonovich's view was typical of the reactions from the left. The radicals
even gave credence to current rumors that Turgenev had planned the whole
novel in cahoots with Katkov simply to denigrate the young. Even Herzen,
although perceptive as ever, thought that Turgenev had initially wished to

praise the "fathers" but had found them so wanting that he had ended up praising the "sons." But Turgenev, he thought, was wrong. If the older generation was fatuous and ineffectual, this did not mean that the young were any better. Destruction may be necessary, but it is not creation. But there was one notable, and unexpected, dissenter among the radicals. Dmitry Pisarev told Turgenev that he had expressed his own opinions in a review of the novel for the journal *Russkoe slovo* (*Russian Word*) with which none of his colleagues agreed. Pisarev was on the left of the political spectrum, but he was not a revolutionary. He believed that Russia could only be saved by the creation of an intellectual elite, and saw Bazarov as its harbinger. Pisarev also maintained that such an elite would come not from the ranks of the gentry, but from the ordinary people. He perceived that throughout the novel Turgenev's sympathies lie clearly on the side of his uncouth but honest and dedicated nihilist, and not with the Kirsanov brothers. "The young people of today are enthusiastic and so fall into extremes," he wrote, "but in their very enthusiasms there is fresh strength and an incorruptible spirit [that] will lead these people on to the right path." A splendid example for others to follow, Bazarov personified what Turgenev himself believed: that change would not come through men like himself, bound as they were by tradition, but through people like Bazarov who are active, unencumbered by the past, and free from all illusions and romantic or religious influences.

Pisarev apart, what really upset most of the younger generation was the fact that Turgenev had made Bazarov purely negative in the sense of purely destructive. The radicals saw nihilism as only a stage in the development of a new type of person, one who would live and die for a cause. Turgenev, they thought, had missed this crucial point.

If the left was almost unanimously hostile, Turgenev received little support from the right either. Most conservatives were alarmed at what they thought he had done, or they found themselves on the defensive. Katkov himself accused Turgenev of glorifying nihilism and pandering to the radicals. He saw Bazarov as towering over all the other characters in the novel and thought Turgenev should have given him opposition worthy of the name. A reactionary like Katkov considered Turgenev's book dangerous to the well-being of Russia. Nikolay Strakhov, although also from a right-wing standpoint, did defend Turgenev against such charges. Turgenev, he said, was only concerned with the truth as he saw it; he wanted to describe reality but not to judge it. If the truth was not always beautiful it was a pity, but that was not Turgenev's concern. Others thought Turgenev had been far too kind to Bazarov, that he had deliberately deemphasized his negative characteristics. He is shown as utterly candid; he has no respect for anything unless he first subjects it to his keen intellect and proves its usefulness; he continuously questions the value of art and literature. All this is in its way admirable, but in the name of what is Bazarov protesting? Science? Knowledge? Progress? But, argued the critics from the right, these are mere words. Bazarov is just putting forth his own propaganda in the place of others'. Bazarov and his ilk are no better than anyone else from the lower ranks of society.

Isaiah Berlin has distinguished at least five distinct reactions among the welter of abuse.[3] There was the angry right-wing brigade who saw Bazarov as an idealized representative of the nihilists whom Turgenev flattered in order to curry favor with the young; some praised him for exposing contemporary barbarism and subversion; others denounced him for his wicked travesty of the radicals; yet others were proud to equate themselves with Bazarov; and finally there were those who were just not sure and thought Turgenev was not certain either. The controversy continues to this day, though now fortunately it is more tempered.

Turgenev was utterly bewildered by his novel's reception. At the time of its publication and on frequent occasions afterward he tried to explain himself, but instead only added to the confusion. Even before allowing it to be printed Turgenev had asked for advice in a futile attempt to please everybody. Even the man Turgenev trusted most, Annenkov, provided little support. He saw Bazarov as a Mongol, a Genghis Khan, a wild beast symptomatic of Russia's savage state. Aleksey Pisemsky thought Bazarov, whatever he was supposed to represent, quite unsuccessful as a literary portrait. Turgenev told Dostoyevski on 30 March 1862, soon after the novel's appearance, that such comments raised doubts in his own mind. His friend, the poet Afanasy Fet, accused him of introspection and tendentiousness. This infuriated Turgenev. "Where, might I ask," he replied angrily from Paris to Fet on 18 April 1862, "is the tendentiousness? . . . Did I want to tear Bazarov to pieces or to extol him? *I don't know that myself.*" Eight days later Turgenev replied at greater length and more calmly to Konstantin Sluchevsky's complaint that there were no positively good people in the novel to counterbalance the others. "Yes," Turgenev insisted, "Bazarov does stand out above all the other characters. . . . I wanted to make him a tragic figure. . . . He is honest and upright, a democrat to his fingertips." If the readers do not love Bazarov, despite his being crude, heartless, pitilessly cold, and abrupt, then, Turgenev admits, he had fallen short of his objective. "I wanted to create a character who was shadowy, strange, life-size, only half-developed, yet strong, fearless, and honest, but nonetheless doomed to failure because he still stands only on the threshold of the future." As for the duel, Turgenev interpreted that as clear proof of the emptiness of the landowning classes: Bazarov gradually destroys Pavel, and the duel is the final stage of the process. And, Turgenev added, though Bazarov calls himself a nihilist for that (although, it might be pointed out, there is hardly a hint of this in the novel) you should read: Revolutionary. What surprised Turgenev the most, however, were not the attacks on Bazarov, but accusations that he supported the "fathers." The whole novel was directed precisely against the gentry as the leading class, he held. Look at its main representatives, Arkady, Nikolay, Pavel: weakness, inertia, limited outlook. Turgenev argued that his aesthetic sense forced him to take precisely the good representatives from the gentry to prove his cases: "If the cream is off, what about the milk?" Such people were the best of the gentry class, and Turgenev highlighted their bankruptcy. Perhaps in that case, Turgenev reports a lady acquaintance of his as remarking, he should have called his book *Neither Fathers nor Sons*. Turgenev did not object. Perhaps the lady was right.

Postscript

Turgenev was so upset by the reception of *Fathers and Sons* that he decided to abandon Russia and Russian literature for good. While he did not carry out this intention entirely, he did live abroad for the rest of his life, and the next three years following the novel's publication were unproductive from a literary point of view. What he did write was profoundly pessimistic and reflected an unhappy period in his life. He completed only three minor short stories, "Ghosts," "Enough," and "The Dog." The first of these was planned in 1855, when he promised it to Katkov for the newly established *Russian Herald*. But he dropped the idea and gave Katkov "Faust" instead. He returned to it after promising Dostoyevski something for his journal *Vremya* (*Time*) and sent it off to Annenkov in September 1863. It was published in Dostoyevski's *Epokha* (*Epoch*), which had succeeded *Vremya* after its suppression by the authorities. It consists of scenes viewed by the narrator when carried through the sky by a mysterious woman, Ellis, a ghost dressed in white, who in the end turns out to be a vampire. The narrator barely manages to stop his nocturnal flights before the bloodsucking to which he has been continually exposed has a fatal effect. The sights the narrator sees are wonderfully described and are both contemporary and historical, for Ellis can fly through both space and time. Many descriptions stem from Turgenev's own experience, for example, those of the Black Forest, Blackgang Rock on the Isle of Wight, Paris, and Lake Maggiore. Historical scenes vary from first-century Rome to a rather brutal episode from the life of the seventeenth-century Russian rebel Stenka Razin. But in the end it all amounts to little more than a series of pictures, as Turgenev later described it. Dostoyevski thought it contained "a lot of rubbish . . . there is something nasty about it, something sick and senile. . . . But poetry will redeem a lot." Fitting Turgenev's mood of the time, "Ghosts" is thoroughly pessimistic, offering no hope at all for the future. Being so depressed himself, he should not really have begun reading Schopenhauer, and there is much of Schopenhauer in "Ghosts."

This applies even more to "Enough," the bleakest story Turgenev ever wrote. Indeed, it is hardly even a story. Subtitled "Fragments from the Notes of a Deceased Painter," it contains fourteen reminiscences of a very unhappy life. Several have to do with a love affair long over. It appears to have been a reciprocated love, but the reader does not know why the affair ended in despair. The main theme is the impotence of man confronted by an implacable, indifferent nature, or what Schopenhauer called the cosmic will. Art provides some consolation, but it is only temporary because nature does not recognize it. Nature "creates even as it destroys but is quite indifferent to *what* it creates or destroys; it is concerned only that life should go on and that death should not lose its rights." All man can do is turn away and cry "enough!" After all he had suffered from friend and foe alike, that is all Turgenev wanted to cry himself.

Chapter Six
The Last Two Novels

Smoke

Smoke, Turgenev's fifth completed novel, appeared in Katkov's *Russian Herald* in the early part of 1867. The idea for the book probably first occurred to him in 1862, immediately after the publication of *Fathers and Sons*. Apparently he originally thought of writing a love story, but his reaction to the reception of *Fathers and Sons* and two developments inside Russia led to a change of emphasis. On a personal level, he became so upset at the hostility directed toward the previous novel and against him personally that he wished to justify himself and perhaps even to pay back his attackers. He was also concerned about the increasingly apparent difficulties with the implementation of the emancipation and over the growing radicalism of the opposition to the czarist government.

Turgenev began writing *Smoke* in November 1864, while staying in Germany at the spa in Baden-Baden. He knew the town extremely well, and in setting his novel there captured its atmosphere very skillfully, depicting the summer visitors, the weather, the surroundings, the hotels and casinos, the avenues and restaurants, as well as the interminable arguments among the Russian residents and holiday-makers. As usual with Turgenev, the plot is uncomplicated. The action occurs over a period of less than a fortnight, from the tenth to the twenty-second of August 1862. The hero, the thirty-year-old Gregory Litvinov, is considered by some of the monstrously conservative Russians there to be "a rebel and free-thinker," but he is actually rather an average man. Litvinov is returning to Russia from Western Europe, where he has been completing his education. He stops in Baden-Baden to await his fiancée Tatyana, who is on her way home with her aunt from holiday. Litvinov meets by chance the novel's heroine, Irina Ratmirova, whom he had known and loved some ten years before and who has since married. He falls in love with her again, and his love is reciprocated. He breaks with Tatyana and begs Irina to go away with him. After much anguish and indecision on both their parts, especially hers, Irina cannot summon the courage to leave the life she knows, and consequently refuses to go. Litvinov returns to Russia a heartbroken and desolate man, despairing about both his own future and that of his country. A few years later, when he has settled down to become a successful farmer, he recovers enough from the episode with Irina to renew his relationship with Tatyana, who forgives him and they marry.

Interspersed throughout *Smoke* are numerous satirical passages describing on the one hand members of the Russian left-wing intelligentsia and on the other reactionary army officers and other influential figures in the social and governmental hierarchy. The counterbalance to them is Potugin, a mouthpiece for many of Turgenev's own most cherished beliefs. Whereas characters, ideas, social background, and behavior were convincingly melded in *Fathers and Sons*, Turgenev never managed to repeat this success in his novels. *Smoke* might mark a significant point in the development of Turgenev's view of life and his opinions about Russia, but in the final analysis it is a rather unfortunate mixture of love story and polemics where neither has much to do with the other. To be sure, almost all the events and the discussions that take place either involve Litvinov or are related through him, and this method does bestow some unity on the novel, but it also imposes serious limits on the scope of the characterization not only of Litvinov but also of the other characters, who, with the exception of Irina, remain rather flat and underdeveloped and tend to become the caricatures with which Turgenev supposedly populated *Fathers and Sons*. Unlike that novel, however, which is a unified and satisfying whole, *Smoke* once again illustrates the difficulties Turgenev had in combining his skill as a storyteller with his wish to comment on contemporary events in his native country.

While the controversy over *Fathers and Sons* was still at its height, and the intensity of the abuse directed at him showed little signs of diminishing, Turgenev wrote to the writer Marko Vovchok on 27 August 1862 that his position inside Russia had become quite untenable, for "despicable generals praised me and the young insulted me." He told the socialist thinker and activist Petr Lavrov that the radicals' attitude to him was unfair and completely unjustified. He saw himself, as he later wrote in "You Will Hear the Judgment of a Fool," one of the late *Prose Poems*, rather like one of his own characters: "Honest souls turned away from him. Honest faces went red with indignation at the very mention of his name." Turgenev patently felt that although he had been misunderstood, he had got himself into rather a false position and did not know how to extricate himself from it except by stopping writing altogether or by leaving Russia for good. Caring less about the opinions of the right-wing although utterly rejecting them (he continually rejected Katkov's suggestions during the writing of *Smoke* that he make all his generals and high-ranking civil servants paragons of virtue), he still thought of himself as a progressive, one of the growing group of people who were determined to change Russia's social and political systems. Yet he could not accept either the behavior displayed by the active radicals or the open contempt in which they held him and his opinions, even though he wanted to portray these same radicals sympathetically too. His exasperation at them was such that all his sympathy for them had evaporated by the time he wrote *Smoke*, in which he attempts to show that his own ideas are important and those of the opposition of little value.

Turgenev told Katkov on 25 December 1866 that *Smoke* would touch on many questions of serious concern to him, and that it would be a tremendously significant work. He would conclude that neither the left nor the right, neither what he saw as the foolish, superficial, muddle-headed, and irresponsible representatives of the young intelligentsia nor yet the unintelligent, ill-informed, blinkered, and pompous bureaucrats and senior army officers, were capable of offering any efficacious remedy for the malaise that gripped Russia. All their talk was just smoke. The despairing Litvinov, on his way back to Russia, muses: "Everything is smoke . . . everything is ceaselessly changing, everywhere there are new forms, event follows event, but essentially everything remains the same; everything rushes and hurries somewhere and everything vanishes without trace, without anything being achieved; another wind may blow and everything then rushes in the opposite direction, and the same ceaseless, restless—and unnecessary—game begins all over again."

Turgenev thought he had a better answer, and when further insults were heaped on him, he was not at all surprised. He told Herzen on 4 June 1867: "They are all attacking me, Reds and Whites, from above and below, and from the sides." He was hardly mistaken, but he himself contributed to his misfortune. Turgenev was, after all, a fine writer of love stories but a poor political pamphleteer, however much he himself thought otherwise while writing the novel. The attempt to combine a pamphlet with a love story proved beyond his capabilities. Yet although *Smoke* does have some faults in construction and characterization, and though some of its conversations and monologues are tedious to read, did it deserve such hostility in Russia? Can it not be read primarily as a love story?

If Turgenev's success at integrating a love story with social and political comment reached its apogee in *Fathers and Sons*, then *Smoke* clearly showed that he was beginning to lose that touch—but he remained as beguiling as ever in composing a love story. The story of Litvinov's passion for Irina, and its unhappy outcome, remains fascinating.

As Litvinov is, as it were, the narrator of everything that happens during that fateful fortnight in Baden-Baden, almost everything that occurs is seen only through his eyes, and consequently his own personality is a little understated. He is a good but very ordinary man, perhaps even rather dull. He is similar in some ways to other male charcters of Turgenev's, to Lezhnev, or Lavretsky, or Arkady Kirsanov, and like them is from the lower ranks of the landowning nobility. His father was a retired civil servant who had married a woman some twenty years younger than he. She had tried to turn him into a landowner rather than a government official (Turgenev always prefers the former to the latter). But neither his mother nor his father did very much about the estate, which remained to all intents and purposes neglected for years. Litvinov was sent to Moscow to study but left before completing his course and returned home, where he developed a passion for farming. Soon realizing that he knew nothing about it, he spent the next four years in Germany, Belgium, and England studying agriculture and technology. He had become engaged to be married to the young Tatyana Shestova, whom he sincerely loved and deeply respected, and at the beginning of the novel is waiting for her arrival in Baden-Baden. He is happy, even serene; his future looks settled and he is proud of his plans for the family estate. But then Irina enters his life for the second time.

Chapters 7–9, in typical Turgenev fashion, depict their previous relationship in Moscow. Some ten years before Litvinov had fallen in love with Irina, the seventeen-year-old daughter of an aristocratic family that had fallen on hard times. Irina was then tall, graceful, intelligent, very beautiful but also temperamental. There was something passionate and self-willed about her, something "that spelled danger for herself and for others." Litvinov fell in love with her at once, but she was slow to return his affection. At the very moment when he decides that his love is hopeless and is about to leave her for ever, she pleads with him to stay. Litvinov always remembered that first occasion when he learned that his love was returned, nor did he forget the days "that came after when still trying to doubt and afraid to believe he clearly saw with a thrill of rapture and almost of awe how the unexpected happiness arose, grew and, sweeping everything before it, flooded his heart at last. There followed the radiant moments of first love, which are not, and indeed ought not to be, repeated in the same life." Weeks and months flew by, not without misunderstandings between the two of them, caused mainly by an apparent inconsistency in Irina's character, coupled with the shame she felt at the comparative poverty in which she and her parents lived. Their relationship ended when Irina attended a ball at which the court was present and made a deep impression on everyone there. Her parents grasped the opportunity, through her, of raising themselves once again into the ranks of the wealthy and influential. They moved to St. Petersburg, where Irina wrote to Litvinov that, however unhappy she felt, all was over between them. "Forgive me, forget me," she urged. "I am not worthy of you. Be generous and do not attempt to see me." Litvinov is heartbroken, for Irina has put material considerations before her love for him. Litvinov abandons his university studies and returns to his father's estate. He gradually loses touch with her and pays no attention to the gossip that reaches his ears from time to time. Irina finally marries general Ratmirov, and Litvinov grows to love Tatyana.

However, the love that flares up again between them becomes an all-consuming passion, especially for Litvinov. For him it is quite simply an obsession, one further complicated by the guilt he feels at rejecting Tatyana, who with both pain and resignation accepts her fate. Finally, after much soul-searching, Litvinov decides he can do nothing but ask Irina to go away with him and share his future, whatever it may bring. Irina is both overjoyed and frightened, but her fear overcomes the uncertain hope of happiness, and she suggests to Litvinov that their commitments are such that they should part. Having resolved to ask Irina to join her life with his, Litvinov is dismayed by her decision, but is prepared to accept it "even if I die afterward." However, later in the day Irina changes her mind and writes to him: "my life is in your hands, do with me what you will. I don't want to hamper your freedom, but if need be I will throw up everything and follow you to the ends of the world." Litvinov then has further doubts himself and entertains dark forebodings at the thought of what happened between them ten years earlier. "Obviously one can't love twice; another life has entered into you—you have allowed it in—and you will never rid yourself of that poison."

The idea of love as sickness is, of course, nothing new in Turgenev, though normally he views the experience of love as an ennobling one. But here the sickness that will pass has become a poison for which there is no antidote. All Litvinov's hopes and ideals, all his plans for the future are destroyed by his passion for Irina. He cannot sleep, he cannot eat, and his powers of rational thought disappear. Things are even worse after their love is passionately consummated. When he makes one last effort to convince her, she, true to her character, first agrees but then tells him that she cannot go with him. She proposes an alternative: that Litvinov come to St. Petersburg, where her influential friends will find him suitable work and they may continue seeing each other. Irina is incapable of living without the support of the society she inhabits, however much she despises many of its values. Such a solution, though, is unacceptable to Litvinov. He leaves for Russia without Irina, not knowing what he will do. "Practical men like Litvinov," as Turgenev sums it up, "should not be carried away by passion; it destroys the very meaning of their lives."

Of all Turgenev's heroines, Irina is certainly the most intriguing. Since readers see her almost entirely through Litvinov's eyes, she remains as mysterious to them as she does to him. She is the first of Turgenev's heroines to possess a demonic quality that clouds her judgment even as it entraps others. More strikingly, she is also the first heroine who ultimately proves weaker than the hero. As she is the most finely drawn and perceptively observed of Turgenev's major heroines, many readers have never forgiven Turgenev for endowing her with the wrong values and yet making her so irresistible. As Edward Garnett wrote: "Irina will stand for ever in the gallery of great creations. Turgenev has in her perfected her type till she reaches a destroying witchery of fascination and subtlety. She ardently desires to become nobler, to possess all that ideal of love . . . but she has only the power given her of enervating the man she loves. She is born to corrupt, but never to be corrupted. Her wit, her scorn, her beauty preserve her from all the influences of evil which she does not deliberately employ."[1]

Remarkably, *Smoke* has a happy ending. After a few years pass Litvinov renews his friendship with Tatyana and asks her to marry him. Her self-sacrifice in releasing him from his earlier promise yields to forgiveness, and she accepts. This strikes the reader as contrived. Turgenev invests all his skill at characterization into Irina, by far the most arresting character in the whole novel. By contrast, Tatyana is a very thinly painted portrait. If Litvinov is distinguished by his mediocrity, then Tatyana seems only virtuous, patient, and long-suffering. Her presence in the novel is largely superfluous, except that she is first the passive cause of Litvinov's mental torment, and then gives him a happy marriage at the last. This does not fit well with what has preceded it. Nor does it contradict Turgenev's generally pessimistic outlook on life. Its artificiality merely demonstrates his inability to believe that any love between a man and a woman can bring anything better than brief happiness. The idea that Tatyana and Irina offer Litvinov the choice between a sacred and a profane love is valid,[2] but it is far too one-sided a contrast to be artistically convincing. It may be not illogical for Litvinov and Tatyana to settle down to an uneventful life together, but Turgenev knew very well that "nature takes no account of logic, of our human logic; she has one of her own, which we do not understand or acknowledge until we are crushed under its wheel." That is the author's authentic voice.

The ideas that Turgenev wished to discuss in *Smoke* have to do either with the future of Russia after the emancipation of the serfs or with the Russian character. Turgenev saw three main options. The first involved major changes suggested by the radical intellectuals and the methods to be employed for their realization; the second was the retention at all costs of the situation as it was thought to be before 1861, the aim of the reactionary generals and bureaucrats; and the third was the middle course that Turgenev himself favored and that he advocated through the character of Potugin. The first two are dismissed with the most biting satire. In the very first chapter Turgenev exposes the boredom, pretentiousness, and emptiness of the Russian upperclass expatriates in Baden-Baden. They fill their time with gambling, gossip, popular music, and meaningless conversations. The opinons of such people—to some of whom Turgenev gives ridiculous names (Prince Koko, Princess Zizi, Princess Zozo) or simply a letter (Countess S, Baron Z, Prince Y)—are fully revealed in chapter 10. Litvinov is taking a leisurely breakfast on the terrace of the Old Castle when a party of Russians arrives. They are all elegantly dressed and converse in French. "Their importance showed itself in everything," Turgenev writes. "The very sound of their voices seemed to be amiably thanking a crowd of subordinates. . . . Each seemed to be deeply conscious of his own dignity and the importance of the part he was to play in the state. . . ." Irina and her husband are among the company, which Litvinov joins, and a conversation develops. A friend of theirs has had to resign his post because he felt he had to justify his high-handed treatment of some tradesman, out of fear of ridicule in the press. A general retorts that if he had his way he would allow the papers to print nothing more than the prices of corn and meat and advertisements for fur coats and boots. "And for the sale of the nobles' estates at auction," adds Irina's husband. This leads on to complaints that the nobility has been ruined by the emancipation, and that it is the job of people such as themselves to stick to their principles and warn the country to stop heading for disaster through reforms. What has been done must be undone, and especially the emancipation, which has brought the landowners nothing but impoverishment. And the peasants? They do not even enjoy their freedom. One of the generals maintains:

"I am not an enemy of so-called progress, but all those universities and seminaries and elementary schools, those students, sons of the clergy, men of no class, all that rabble. . . . Yes, we must draw the line. Bear in mind no one in Russia asks for anything or makes any demands. Self-government, for instance, is anyone asking for it? Do you ask for it? Or you? Or you? You rule not only over yourselves, but over all of us as it is." (The general's face was lit up by an amused smile.) "Democracy is glad to welcome you, it flatters you, it is ready to serve your ends, but it is a double-edged weapon. Much better to have things done in the old, well-tried way. Don't allow the mob to get presumptuous but trust to the aristocracy, which alone is strong. . . . And as for progress—I really have nothing against it. Only don't give us all those lawyers and juries and elected rural officials—and above all don't interfere with discipline—as for the rest, you may build bridges and wharves and hospitals, and there is no harm in lighting the streets with gas."

In other words, keep things exactly as they used to be, but allow a little social improvement. Turgenev's contempt for such people and their opinions is expressed not only in the satirical presentation but also through Litvinov, who, we read, "could not have picked out a single sincere word, a single sensible idea or new fact from all that dull and incomprehensible babble. There was no real excitement in their shouts and exclamations, no passion in their censure; only sometimes the fear of financial loss. And not a drop of living water under all that litter and rubbish. What stale trash, what worthless trifles, what barren futilities. . . . And at bottom, what ignorance!" Even Irina agrees with him. The people in her world, she tells Litvinov, "understand nothing, they have no sympathy for anything, they haven't even intelligence, only *savoir faire* and cunning, [and] they don't care a scrap for music or art or poetry." Litvinov's honest plebeian pride is aroused and he wonders what he, the son of a petty official, could possibly have in common with these St. Petersburg military aristocrats. Everything he believed in was diametrically opposed to their views: Litvinov "thought their jokes flat, their tone unendurable, their movements affected. The very softness of their speech suggested to him a revolting contemptuousness." And clearly Turgenev agreed with his hero.

If Turgenev dismisses the reactionary view, he does the same for the radicals. If the left-wing had criticized Bazarov for being a caricature when he was not, then here Turgenev shows what he was capable of in this area. His contempt for the radical stance emerges most clearly in chapter 4, describing a group led by Gubarev (whose prototype is probably Herzen's friend and collaborator Ogarev), who voices their political aims. They must study the peasantry, he says, unite with it, and find out what it really thinks. Gubarev considers the peasantry a revolutionary force. But Turgenev ridicules Gubarev and his ideas no less energetically than he does those of the rightwing. His view of the peasantry is shown as absurdly romantic; he and his followers are drawn as insincere, shallow, and wrong-headed. Turgenev surrounds Gubarev with a motley crew of nonentities as if to stress that point: there are the empty-headed Bambaev, the glory-seeking Bindasov, the gossiping and opinionated Voroshilov (who, Turgenev told Annenkov, casts dust in people's eyes by quoting the latest pronouncements of science without knowing what went before), the misguided Pishchalkin, and the silly

Madame Sukhanchikova, who exists on a diet of half-baked ideas, ill-digested opinions, and the juiciest of scandals. Turgenev is as severe on these characters and what they purport to stand for as he is on the reactionaries. Both camps are equally ridiculous but, in Turgenev's opinion, if not shown up for what they really are, both are equally dangerous for the future well-being of Russia.

Potugin advocates a middle way. His position in the novel is as artistically tenuous as Tatyana's, and although Turgenev tries to integrate him into the love story by casting him as Irina's selfless and devoted admirer who carries out her every wish (including spying on Litvinov), he does not succeed. Potugin has no real place in the story of Litvinov's passion for Irina, and his long speeches on Russia and its future simply delay the development of the narrative. But as a mouthpiece for Turgenev's own ideas, he is of prime importance.

Potugin comes from the *raznochintsy*. The son of a priest, he is full of down-to-earth common sense, and has had long experience of the workings of the bureaucracy. Life, however, has not treated him at all kindly, and he is now a lonely and embittered man. But he is also a man of conviction, a Westernizer. Turgenev wrote to Pisarev on 4 June 1867 from Baden-Baden: "In common with most of my Russian readers you do not like *Smoke*. In the face of such a unanimous response I cannot but doubt the qualities of my creation . . . But from the heights of European civilization one can still survey the whole of Russia. You think that Potugin is Arkady all over again. I cannot but say that here your critical sense has deserted you—these two characters have absolutely nothing in common. Arkady has no convictions whatsoever, while Potugin will die an inveterate and passionate Westernizer, and my writings will all have been in vain if this fierce and inextinguishable fire does not come through."

According to Potugin, Russians have two major difficulties. They have an innate need to be led, and it has not mattered much by whom. That is why the left-wing has its Gubarevs: the important thing is not his ideas as such, but rather his strength of will and ability to convince others of the correctness of his opinions. The second problem is the Russian attitude toward Western Europe. The Russians might argue that Europe has run its historical course, but it still provides the intellectual nourishment on which Russia will survive and flourish. Neither the generals' wish to return to some mystic Russia of long ago—preferably as long ago as possible—nor the left-wing's romantic dreams of the revolutionary potential of the peasantry, will help. What is needed is a selective borrowing from the very best that Western Europe has to offer. Russians cannot help themselves by their own resources. History, according to Potugin, emphasizes this simple fact, however much most of his countrymen fail to recognize it. What has Russia ever produced of any lasting value to mankind? In painting, only the insignificant Bryullov; in music, Glinka is perhaps the exception, which only shows up the poverty of his predecessors; in science and industry, nothing. Even the samovar, bast shoes, and the knout, those apparently quintessentially Russian items, were all imported from abroad. Russians must show more humility. Unable to understand simple facts, they concoct theories that lead only to idealistic conclusions of no help to anyone, least of all the Russians themselves. "We must thank civilization," Potugin says, "not only for knowledge, art, and law but even for the idea of beauty itself and of poetry . . . and the people's so-called naive and unconscious art is all stuff and nonsense."

At the very end of the novel, as Litvinov sets out for Russia, Potugin bids him farewell with the advice: "Each time you begin something new, ask yourself whether you are serving civilization . . . whether your activity is of the educative, European kind, which alone is useful and fruitful in our times and for us." That is Potugin's message, and also Turgenev's, one he delivered consistently throughout his life.

Virgin Soil

Turgenev's last and longest novel is usually regarded as a *roman à thèse*, and so largely disregarded. D. S. Mirsky, for example, dismisses it in the following words: "*Virgin Soil* is a complete failure and was immediately recognized as such. Though it contains much that is in the best manner of Turgenev . . . the whole novel is disqualified by an entirely uninformed and necessarily false conception of what he was writing about. His presentation of the revolutionaries of the seventies is like an account of a foreign country by one who had never seen it."[3] Richard Freeborn entitles his chapter on the novel "The Failure of *Virgin Soil*."[4]

Turgenev was well aware of the difficulties of writing about Russia while living abroad. He admitted that one cannot attempt to expose the essence of Russia while living almost permanently abroad. He had taken up a task far beyond his powers. He thought that the fate of any Russian writer of prominence contained a tragic element. His was absenteeism. Such opinions engendered many forebodings. Was Turgenev really out of touch with Russia? Had his ability as a novelist declined even further after *Smoke*? Must *Virgin Soil* be discounted as ill-informed, poorly written, and adding nothing of interest to our knowledge of Turgenev? Most of his readers have been rather disappointed in it, despite its immediate popularity outside Russia. They think they perceive an evident decline in his powers as a writer, as a commentator on contemporary events in Russia, as a creator of unforgettable characters, and as a weaver of stories, especially love stories. Yet Turgenev himself, despite the volume of negative critical comment, was convinced that ultimately his novel would be useful to his country.

Virgin Soil springs from Turgenev's interest in the early stages, dating from the late 1860s, of the so-called movement to the people and his judgment upon it. The purpose of the movement, which culminated in a massive exodus from the towns to the countryside by idealistic young students and others in the summer of 1874, was to spread revolutionary propaganda amongst the ordinary people by attempting to share their lives and thus their problems. Ultimately they hoped to incite the peasantry to oppose the landowners, factory owners, the authorities, and the czarist government. Their ideas of what would replace the established social, political, and economic order were couched in rather vague and even inconsistent terms, including utopian socialism, anarchism, even a form of enlightened, but temporary, dictatorship. Initially the call "go to the people; that is where you belong" had come from Herzen—and is critically reflected in Gubarev's beliefs in *Smoke*. Bakunin had thought the conditions of the peasantry so awful and their hatred of the government so deep that they could easily be stirred into revolt with the right leadership. Petr Lavrov added fuel to the fire through his *Istoricheskie pisma* (*Historical Letters*), published at the end of the 1860s, in which he wrote of the debt owed to the people by the intelligentsia, or in other words the gentry. This was the birth of the concept of the "repentant nobleman." But by the end of 1874 the enthusiasm, idealism, and dedication of youth lay in ruins. Government authorities employed all the means at their disposal in retaliation and arrested well over a thousand people for spreading revolutionary propaganda. More important, perhaps, was the often suspicious attitude of the peasants themselves, who rejected the young intellectuals who tried to dress as they did and live with them. The mutual misunderstanding was pronounced, as the peasants either refused to listen to the strangers in their midst or handed them over to the police. The movement culminated in the "Trial of the 193" which marked the end of this particular phase of Russian populism. Turgenev reflects all of this in *Virgin Soil*.

Turgenev first mentioned a book on this latest phenomenon in Russian society as early as July 1870, when he sketched out a short list of characters contrasting a "romantic revolutionary" (Nezhdanov) with a more realistic man who goes calmly about his work (Solomin). For the next few years the idea germinated gradually, until on 27 July 1876 he wrote to his editor Mikhail Stasyulevich (by this time he had fallen out with Katkov), publisher of the journal *Vestnik Evropy* (*Messenger of Europe*), that his new novel would be called *Virgin Soil* and bear the epigraph: "To turn over virgin soil it is necessary to use a deep plow going well into the earth, not a surface one gliding lightly over the top." Turgenev insisted, however, that his plow was a metaphor not for revolution but for enlightenment. The manuscript was completed in November 1876. Turgenev feared that the novel would be badly received, and that if he had been beaten for *Fathers and Sons* with sticks then it would be tree-trunks this time. He was not mistaken. At the end of 1876 Turgenev wrote to Stasyulevich:

Up until now the younger generation has either been represented in our literature as a gang of crooks and rogues, which is false and could only insult the young reader as a lie and a libel, or it has been idealized, which again is false, and, besides, harmful. I decided to approach the truth along the middle way—to depict young people, most of them good and honest, and to show that notwithstanding their disinterestedness the task that they had set themselves was so artificial and untrue to life that it could only end in fiasco. . . . Whatever happens, the young cannot possibly complain that they have been depicted by an enemy; on the contrary, I think that they cannot but feel the sympathy I have if not for their aims then at least for them personally. It is in this way that a novel written for them and about them can be useful to them.

For all that, when the novel appeared in the early part of 1877 it was received as Turgenev had feared. Almost no one in Russia liked it. The right wing attacked him for his adverse comments on Russia, and for his highly satirical portrayal of the Sipyagin family and of Kallomeytsev. The left wing could not countenance his making his "hero" Nezhdanov so irresolute and feeble, or Marianna not determined enough and prey to her emotions, or Solomin too "bourgeois." But there was another and more justifiable reason for the attacks. In 1877 *Virgin Soil* could be thought several years out of date, for the Populist movement, upon recovering from the debacle Turgenev describes so well, had entered a more radical and violent stage.

The "story" in *Virgin Soil* is the most complex Turgenev ever attempted; the book contains many minor characters and subsidiary plots. It combines two romantic love stories with Turgenev's analysis of the revolutionary movement of the late 1860s (although much of what he wrote applied equally well to the mid-1870s). The love elements, though, do appear to be rather a side issue and have very little to do with the novel's main message. *Virgin Soil* opens at the lodgings of some Russian revolutionaries. One of them, Mashurina—an intense, rather unattractive young woman—is shown as a dedicated follower of a certain Vasily Nikolaevich, a shadowy figure who never appears but who is clearly modeled on the revolutionary Sergey Nechaev, whose long trial in 1871–73 Turgenev followed closely. Not all the group, however, obey his every command. Nezhdanov, the ostensible hero (with whom Mashurina is obviously although secretly in love), is far too introspective and skeptical to follow anyone blindly. The illegitimate son of a wealthy nobleman, he is employed by Sipyagin as tutor to his son. Sipyagin is portrayed throughout the novel in disapproving terms. He is an influential, ambitious government official, determined to appear liberal but actually ever loyal to the government. Clearly he lives by self-interest, and is at heart a hypocrite and snob.

Sipyagin's neighbor Kallomeytsev is painted with particular venom as an out-and-out reactionary with pretensions, and at times his characterization lapses into caricature. Sipyagin's wife Valentina Mikhaylovna is a self-possessed, cold-hearted, vain, and capricious woman. She has pretentions to culture just as her husband has to liberalism, but she is merciless toward those of weaker character than she and at a loss with those of stronger character. Her brother, Markelov, is markedly different. He is a fanatical revolutionary, convinced that the Russian peasantry only need a "spark" to set off the fires of revolt. When his activities inevitably lead to his arrest (his brother-in-law, far from helping him, actually assists in the process) he refuses to name any of his collaborators and acts with admirable courage and dignity. He is in love with Marianna, the novel's heroine, but his affection is not returned. Marianna, Valentina Mikhaylovna's niece, has been brought up in her household. Never allowed to forget the generosity of the Sipyagins, she dislikes and despises her "benefactors" and yearns for freedom and activity. She and Nezhdanov are immediately attracted to each other although she loves the cause he is fighting for more than she loves him, and wants to join her life to his in order to serve the people. She is typical of many young women of the period—idealistic, dedicated, and rather naive—but Turgenev fails to make her other than a representative type or to endow her with the psychological depth of his great heroines. She is certainly not as pale a creation as Natalya in *Rudin* but she does not begin to compare with either Liza (*Home of the Gentry*) or, especially in this context, with Elena (*On the Eve*). Similarly, Nezhdanov recalls some of Turgenev's earlier ineffectual heroes. He is as unsure of his dedication to the revolutionary cause as he is of his love for Marianna.

From the very earliest drafts of the novel Turgenev intended that Nezhdanov should end his life in despair and by his own hand. The weakness in the characterization of Nezhdanov—who remains nonetheless the most interesting character in the whole novel—is a weakness of *Virgin Soil* as a whole. In his plan of 1872 Turgenev describes him as "a tragic nature with a tragic destiny." He should have embodied the tragic destiny of a whole generation, but as things turned out his tragedy is not that of his generation but a personal one. It is almost as if Turgenev reverted one last time to the "superfluous man." He is as Paklin describes him in the last chapter: a "splendid fellow" but an "idealist of realism." He was simply not fit to be a revolutionary. He was rather an aristocrat manqué who longed to be a peasant democrat, a poet not an activist. Nezhdanov should dominate the novel, but, to its detriment, he never does.

Nezhdanov and Marianna finally escape together from the Sipyagin household. They are offered help by the novel's real hero, Solomin, the manager of a local factory who provides them with shelter and contact with the local peasantry. Solomin himself has little faith in revolutionary activity but is prepared to protect and assist those who do. From the start Turgenev wanted to contrast Solomin and Nezhdanov, the practical man and the dreamer. The son of a clergyman, Solomin studied science and mathematics and worked in England. He remains aloof from those who preach revolution because he does not think the ordinary people either understand it or want it. He believes in slow and patient work, as Turgenev stresses in contrasting his way of life with Nezhdanov's. When the latter dresses as an ordinary workman and distributes revolutionary literature among the peasants, his misguided efforts end in abject failure. Enticed into the local taverns, he quickly becomes hopelessly intoxicated and is brought home in a state of collapse. The sight of him even shakes for a time Marianna's belief in the people: "She was not disturbed but depressed. It seemed as if a breath of the real atmosphere of the world to which she was striving had blown upon her suddenly, making her shudder at its coarseness and darkness. What Moloch was this to which she was going to sacrifice herself?"

This is, however, only a temporary lapse. Solomin even persuades her that she can be of far more use to the people, not by becoming "simplified" herself, in the words of a peasant employee of his (an expression that Turgenev had heard from one of his own peasants at Spasskoe) or by handing out literature to illiterate peasants, but by undertaking something far humbler: nursing the local children and teaching them to read. Marianna is disappointed but agrees with the practicality of his suggestion. When, later, Markelov is arrested, suspicion falls upon Nezhdanov, Marianna, and Solomin, with no little help from Sipyagin. Nezhdanov finally capitulates to his doubts, writes a letter to Solomin and Marianna urging them to marry each other, and shoots himself. His motivation has nothing to do with fear of arrest or its consequences, but stems from the continual indecision he had shown throughout his short life, his inability to convince himself of the rightness of his cause, his guilt at being (at least partially) from the aristocracy, and his uncertainty as to whether his love for Marianna is genuine. There are also a few hints to show that he suspects Solomin, who loves Marianna himself, is the better man for her. After his death Marianna and Solomin go into hiding until the affair dies down. They will shortly marry and, presumably, continue to work together for the cause to which Solomin has dedicated himself.

Although *Virgin Soil* is occasionally tedious to read—some repetitive pages could easily have been omitted without detriment to the rest—and the characterization less full and more stereotyped than is normally the case with Turgenev, it is clear that Turgenev has finally abandoned the belief that his own class would produce the likely leaders of reform in Russia. Earlier he had repeatedly argued that Russia's educated class was her only hope of salvation. He always rejected violence as pointless, indeed positively harmful, and believed Russia could never be reformed except from above. His high hopes for the emancipation of the serfs ten years later were disappointed. *Virgin Soil*, despite its defects, shows that his faith now lay in men and women from a different social background from his own, men like Solomin, practical, enterprising, and ambitious, but also patient, realizing that change will take time. As he points out: "The main thing about [Solomin] is that he is no instant healer of all our social ills. Just look at us Russians—we are always waiting. Something or someone will always turn up—and cure everything at a stroke. Who will this magician be? Darwinism? The village? A foreign war? Anything you like." But Solomin is prepared to wait and to work for gradual but certain improvement.

Although Turgenev portrays the "movement to the people" as naive and a little absurd, he also believed that those who participated in it were redeemed by their devotion to their beliefs. Although the young disliked his portrayal of them, he was surely sympathetic to them—for their faith, their sincerity, and their willing self-sacrifice. As Paklin puts it at the very end of the novel, it is people like Solomin who will make the future, they are the real men. "They're strong, colorless, dull men of the people. But now they're the only kind that's needed." He is a man with an ideal and yet sensible; an educated man, yet one from the ordinary people. Turgenev could admire such a man and prophesy that the future was his. It might be said that he was right.

Chapter Seven

The Final Years

Miscellaneous Memoirs

During the last decade or so of his life Turgenev continued to publish stories, but at irregular intervals. Despite his attempt to deal with contemporary Russia in *Virgin Soil*, after his unhappy experiences with *Fathers and Sons* and especially with *Smoke* he largely turned his back on current social and political questions. He is still at his very best in some of what he published then—"The Torrents of Spring" and a few of the short stories—but in general the later works are of lower quality and less interest. Their mood is one of nostalgic regret, and Turgenev's pessimism about the human condition intensified. As the narrator of "Punin and Baburin" remarks: "I am old and ill and think mostly of death, which draws nearer with every day. . . . Only occasionally do I recall bygone years, happenings, faces; but then my thoughts do not dwell on the prime of my life or on my young manhood. They carry me back to my early childhood." Yet the former Turgenev is still apparent as earlier themes and preoccupations reappear, though now with a slightly different emphasis. Furthermore, although he had always asserted that he had no interest in the supernatural, some of his best later stories contain a strong element of the fantastic or the mysterious.

As perhaps a reflection of his mood, this period witnesses the appearance of some of his memoirs. In 1869 he published a series of five articles: a general "Introduction," his "Reminiscences of Belinsky," reflections on the writers Gogol, Zhukovsky, Krylov, Lermontov, and Zagoskin, "A Literary Party at P. A. Pletnev's," in which he describes, among other things, his two brief meetings with his lifelong idol Pushkin, and a defense of *Fathers and Sons*. He later added a description of a visit to Italy with his friend Vasily Botkin, first published in 1861, and a charming, albeit rather technical, study called "Nightingales," written for Sergey Aksakov's sporting memoirs in 1855. Of the other items in the collection as it is known today, two deal with events during the 1848 uprising in Paris—the story "Chelovek v serykh ochkakh" ("The Man in the Grey Spectacles"), unsuccessful because it carries little conviction and the personality of its leading character is rather flat, and the much better "Nashi poslali!" ("My Comrades Sent Me"), with its vivid description of those stormy days.

By far the most impressive reminiscence of all is the hauntingly memorable "Kazn' Tropmana" ("Execution of Tropman"). In January 1870 the twenty-one-year-old Jean-Baptiste Tropman was guillotined for the murder of an entire family. A friend of Turgenev's had invited him to spend the night before the execution in the prison to watch the preparations and then to witness the execution the following morning. Turgenev did not wish to go, but agreed in order not to appear a coward. His picture of the gruesome occasion does not shield the reader from any of its horrifying details, and the effect is powerful. He hoped the story would be published and given as wide a circulation as possible because he hoped it would provide arguments for those in favor of the abolition of capital punishment.

Two other stories of this period reflect Turgenev's passion for shooting game and for the Russian countryside: "Pegaz" ("Pegasus"), a description of one of his favorite game dogs, and, "Perepelka" ("The Quail," 1883). The latter contains a few biographical details but is notable as the only story Turgenev ever wrote specifically for children. Produced at the request of Tolstoy's wife, it was included in a volume of children's stories, the others being written by Tolstoy himself. Turgenev was flattered, but worried that his charming story of a dying bird would suffer by appearing "in such close proximity" to Tolstoy's work. "My 'Quail' has been greatly honored," he wrote to Tolstoy in the last months of his life. However keen a sportsman Turgenev might have been, "The Quail" shows clearly that he always regretted the suffering inflicted upon game birds by man in the pursuit of pleasure.

The last story to be included in the collection was "A Fire at Sea," which Turgenev, too ill to write, dictated to Pauline Viardot just before he died. It records an incident that occurred when he was traveling to Germany by sea at nineteen. The boat caught fire and, according to most accounts, some of which might well have been true, Turgenev was caught up in the general panic and did not display great bravery. Although his final recollection is fictionalized and a little embellished, it is a last exorcism of an event he had never forgotten and of which he was no doubt on occasion ashamed.

Short Stories

The stories "Brigadir" ("The Brigadier"), "Istoriya leytenanta Ergunova" ("The Story of Lieutenant Ergunov"), "Neschastnaya" ("An Unhappy Girl"), "Strannaya istoriya" ("A Strange Story"), "Stepnoy korol' Lir" ("A King Lear of the Steppes"), "Stuk . . . stuk . . . stuk" ("Knock . . . Knock . . . Knock"),

"Punin and Baburin," and "Chasy" ("The Watch"), all published between 1868 and 1876, reflect Turgenev's nostalgic mood. They are all set in the past, and many of them contain autobiographical elements.

"The Brigadier" (1868) is based on a letter Turgenev found amongst his mother's papers at Spasskoe. An elderly army officer who had made his career during the Napoleonic Wars is living in poverty in the country. He writes to the niece of a rich woman landowner asking for help and shelter. In his younger days he had been deeply in love with the landowner and had given her years of selfless devotion. It is a slight tale, but the letter itself, written in Turgenev's best style, is very moving. The story also avoids any sentimentality, as Turgenev always sought to do.

Although published in the same year, "The Story of Lieutenant Ergunov" is of more interest. It was written while Turgenev was finishing *Smoke*, and although it took him some time to complete, when composing it he showed his usual facility: he even boasted that he wrote the last twenty pages "in one day." When he finished it, in Baden-Baden, he told Pauline Viardot that it had turned out longer than he had originally planned, and it is clear that he took considerable care with the characterization of its two leading personages. He took the manuscript with him on one of his periodic visits to Russia and read it to friends who, while generally approving it, suggested some changes, for example, that he broaden the character of the "heroine" and tone down what some might consider the "immoral" nature of certain passages.

The story takes place at the end of the 1820s in the port of Nikolaev, a relatively new town founded in 1789, which, incidentally, Turgenev had never visited. It describes an incident in the life of the young Lieutenant Ergunov, one he was always ready to recall to anyone prepared to listen. Twenty-five at the time, Ergunov was placed in charge of the building of the shipyards in Nikolaev. Though inexperienced and something of a dandy, he was a prudent and trustworthy young man. He never played cards or drank, and shunned the company of others: he found his only pleasure in taking solitary evening strolls around the town, admiring the flowers and sighing after young ladies he saw. He had a weakness for the fair sex, but he had never permitted himself any "foolishness." That he should succumb to temptation is not at all surprising.

One evening, while out walking in the town, he meets a distraught young woman who tells him that a cook has stolen all her possessions and that the police take no interest in her case. She is supposedly Emiliya Karlovna, nineteen, very good-looking and flirtatious. She takes him to her dismal home where he is introduced to Madam Fritsche, an unprepossessing Jewess who is apparently Emiliya's aunt. Later a man surreptitiously delivers a parcel that

Ergunov thinks might have traces of blood on it. Emiliya, very defensive, claims that no men come to the house. The mystery deepens when Ergunov thinks he sees the man again as he leaves. He takes to visiting the house frequently, but the two (or is it more?) residents tell him nothing about themselves, and he never enters any other rooms but the one in which they receive him. On one occasion he falls asleep and suspects that Emiliya has tampered with his money belt; on another Emiliya invites him to the house, although she later denies it, and he meets someone said to be Emiliya's younger sister, the seductive Kolibri (in Russian: a hummingbird) who flirts with him, sings and dances, tempts the impressionable young man but permits him no more than a fleeting kiss. She is as mysterious about her life and the house as the others. While Ergunov is powerfully drawn to her, there is here no element comparable to those in certain other Turgenev stories, where the hero finds himself in the throes of an uncontrollable passion which leads to disaster. On another day Ergunov drinks a glass of drugged tea and gradually falls asleep, to dream, peacefully and serenely, of going with Kolibri to Turkey, and then to awaken in a hospital. The transition from reality to dream, the description of the dream itself, and the return to consciousness is extremely well done, and Turgenev was especially proud of these passages.

In the end the mystery is to a large extent cleared up. Ergunov had been drugged, robbed, beaten over the head, and left for dead by the man he had seen on his first visit to the house. It transpires that the four residents of the house are all on the run from the police, that their true names are not those given to Ergunov, that the man is a violent thief, and that the two girls are used by him and Madam Fritsche as bait for unsuspecting people, and that Emiliya and Kolibri are probably prostitutes as well.

The story was poorly received in Russia. "A very ordinary tale," the critics remarked: "Turgenev has regressed. The same marvelous style—but that's all"; "We expect more from Turgenev than empty, stale, old anecdotes." Even the praise was at best ironic: as the critic for one newspaper wrote, "only such a fine and subtle writer as Turgenev could have made such an elegant, artistic tale out of such empty subject matter." Although the story contains much that is typical of Turgenev, and even typical of him at his best, it is difficult to gainsay the contemporary critics. Turgenev always had difficulties with sheer invention. His best and most enduring works are based to a greater or lesser extent on his own experience or that of others about which he knew.

Turgenev was extremely sensitive when questioned about his attitude toward the Jews, and always claimed he bore them no ill will. They appear infrequently in his stories, but the stereotyped characters in the early "The Jew" and the profession of the two Jewesses in "Lieutenant Ergunov" lent support to those who suspected he was tinged with anti-Semitism. "An Unhappy Girl" (1869), though, provides ample evidence to the contrary. It was written in Spasskoe, while Turgenev was on one of his regular visits to Russia and when, he admitted, he was overwhelmed by love for his native country and by memories of his youth. As in his first published story, "Andrey Kolosov," he returns to his student days in Moscow when he first heard a similar story. The heroine, Susanna, is the illegitimate daughter of a landowner who never acknowledges her. He marries off her mother, a Jewess, who soon dies, leaving Susanna at the mercy of a sadistic stepfather. A love affair develops between Susanna and the son of her real father's brother. Simply because Susanna is a Jewess, the two older men attempt to hinder the young couple at every step. Susanna dies very suddenly, but the cause of her death is unclear: she might have died of natural causes, committed suicide, or been poisoned by her stepfather, who will inherit her income. Turgenev exhibits his usual skill at drawing convincing characters and recapturing the atmosphere of the past. Susanna's Jewishness is very finely detailed, and the manuscripts show that Turgenev went to much trouble to get it right. Susanna emerges as an extremely sympathetic character, in marked contrast to the few other Jews in his fiction, who are at best rather inferior people. Susanna's unhappy life and untimely death are the result primarily of her Jewish descent, a fact which engenders outrage in the reader's mind.

Throughout his career Turgenev had been interested in Russia's religious dissenters, the Old Believers, as we see from characters such as Kasyan in *A Sportsman's Sketches* or Akim in "The Inn." He was not at all concerned with their theological convictions, but rather with the social or moral problems they posed. In 1868 he drew up a plan for a long historical novel to be based on the seventeenth-century Old Believer priest Nikita of Suzdal, known to his detractors as Pustosvyat (His Holynothingness). Nothing came of this idea, but in 1870 Turgenev did publish a slight tale, "A Strange Story," in which the daughter of a rich landowner, inspired by deep humility and Christian ethics, abandons a life of ease to devote herself to one of the uneducated "holy men" who wandered about the country living on charity. Although it does highlight the difficulties of the dissenters and present a picture of certain traits Turgenev admired in Russian women, it is ultimately no more than a frightful picture of particular aspects of Russian life.

The lesser known story "Knock . . . Knock . . . Knock" (1871) deserves attention for a number of reasons. It reflects Turgenev's views on the romanticism of the late 1820s and the 1830s and on what might be called the original "superfluous man," characters such as the heroes of Alexander Marlinsky's long-forgotten novels, Pushkin's Onegin, and Lermontov's

Pechorin. "All sorts of elements were mingled in that type," says the narrator. "Byronism, romanticism, memories of the French revolution, of the Decembrists—and the worship of Napoleon; faith in destiny, in one's star, in strength of will; posing and fine phrases—and a miserable sense of the emptiness of life; uneasy pangs of petty vanity—and genuine strength and bravery; generous impulses, and defective education, ignorance; aristocratic airs, and delight in trivial foppery. . . ."

Turgenev's embodiment of such a "fatalist" is Lieutenant Teglev, whose story is told by his friend Ridel. In the 1830s Ridel used to visit his brother in Krasnoe Selo, near St. Petersburg, where he was stationed as a cavalry officer. There he meets Teglev, a man who believes passionately in "fate." Despite all appearances to the contrary, he firmly believes that he is destined to play a significant part in life. His conviction of his own greatness drives him to adopt the role of a "fatalist," which he supports by undertaking various "heroic" adventures. On the eve of Teglev's name-day Ridel spends the night in his house. Teglev tells him of certain occurrences, forebodings, and apparitions that he interprets as ill omens. As he prepares to sleep Ridel knocks on the hollow wall of his room for no apparent reason. Teglev interprets the knocking as a message from his former girlfriend Masha, whom he has deserted. Teglev goes out into the night looking for Masha's "ghost," hears a voice whispering his name, and is convinced that Masha has killed herself. The following day he receives confirmation of his worst fears and decides that he must follow her example. In the evening he gives Ridel a letter for his commanding officer and vanishes into the thick mist of the summer's night to commit suicide. Ridel tries to prevent this foolish act, but fails. Ridel later discovers that Masha has indeed died, but from cholera, and that the voice calling Teglev's name had been that of another woman looking for her lover, who happened to have the same first name as Teglev. The story ends on a melancholy note: "Yes, someone has observed truly of those who commit suicide: until they carry out their plan, no one believes them; and when they do, no one regrets them."

Throughout his adult life Turgenev had been concerned with what he saw as irrational elements in human life. As a child he had been aware of his parents' belief in ill omens. He often said that he had experienced telepathy, prophetic dreams, and forebodings in his own life. While spending the summer with the Viardots in France in 1849, he fell prey continually to strange sensations. None of these experiences boded, he believed, anything but ill. Such phenomena recur throughout his shorter stories, and they lend an air of inevitability to many events he describes.

A premonition that Teglev's life will end badly lies at the core of "Knock

... Knock ... Knock." The episode of the knocking occurs on Teglev's name-day, a fact to which he attaches the utmost importance. This feeling is reinforced by the fact that he has also that day given alms to an old woman who had promised "to pray for his soul." As Teglev begins to expect some fateful happening, even Ridel, who at first laughs at the "boring fatalist," is infected by his mood and feels something akin to compassion for Teglev. He discounts his faith in the destiny that rules his life as an affected pose, but still senses that some tragic fate did await him. And that turns out to be the case. Teglev might have died from "fatalism," or from his own foolishness; he might even have shared the death wish apparent in Pechorin's final days, but in spite of everything his forebodings of his own death prove accurate. However rational an explanation Turgenev might have provided for Teglev's visions, and however much the reader may wonder whether Teglev was predisposed to suicide or whether he was indeed under the sway of evil forces, the outcome still appears inevitable.

While the story did not attract much favorable criticsm, Turgenev could not entirely agree with, say, Annenkov, who thought it altogether one of his lesser pieces. As Turgenev wrote to a correspondent in January 1877, "I consider the story successful—even if it does leave something to be desired and is a little weak. It is one of the most serious things I've ever written. It is a study of suicide, in particular of a contemporary, Russian kind—proud, meaningless, superstitious—and empty and ridiculous."

Turgenev's tendency during his later years to look at Russia's history emerges particularly in "The Watch" (1876) and "Punin and Baburin" (1874). The leading characters in both stories are two friends who recall Bazarov and Arkady in *Fathers and Sons* in the sense that one is distinctly dominant over the other. "The Watch," a sort of picaresque parable, is set at the turn of the nineteenth century, during the reigns of Paul and Alexander I. The narrator receives a watch from his godfather, a corrupt government official. At first he is delighted with it, until a cousin—whose father has been exiled to Siberia for his radical activities and republican opinions—tells him the watch is no good, and that anyway he should not accept gifts from such a man as his godfather. The rest of the story details the boy's attempts to get rid of the watch, by hiding it, burying it, or giving it away. But it is all to no avail, because either pressure from his family and friend, or his own pride of possession compels him to retrieve it. In addition to demonstrating Turgenev's skill at recalling the past and his ability to enter into the mind of a young boy, the story might also be interpreted on a metaphorical level. The watch might represent Russia's existing social system, or else the corruption of the "old" Russia. The watch is finally disposed of by the republican-minded cousin, who throws it into a river but nearly drowns in the process. The allegorical meanings are clear.

Whether this view of "The Watch" is sustainable or not, the radical theme of "Punin and Baburin" is clearly central to it. The story is related by Petya, the young grandson of a tyrannical woman landowner, in four historical periods: 1830, 1837, 1849, and 1861. The first narration recalls Turgenev's own boyhood at Spasskoe. Baburin, appointed a clerk on an estate, brings his friend Punin with him. Punin is a gentle man who loves reciting poetry and stories that enchant the young narrator, whereas the strong-willed Baburin holds "republican" views: he opposes the arbitrary power landowners exercise over their serfs, and is himself before long dismissed.

The second section is set seven years later, when Petya is a second-year university student. A friend of Petya's, Tarkhov, is in love with Musa, an eighteen-year-old seamstress. It soon transpires that Musa is an orphan, and also illegitimate like Baburin, who has taken her under his wing in the same philanthropic spirit that moved him to support Punin. He is prepared to marry Musa but at the time she prefers Tarkhov and Baburin accepts her choice.

Twelve years later at Punin's funeral Petya again meets Baburin, now aged considerably and married to Musa. She is calmer and more determined, having lost what Petya calls her "vanity," or in other words her egoism and her belief that love is the most important thing in life. When Baburin is arrested and exiled, Musa accompanies him. Although Turgenev does not say so, evidently Baburin was marginally involved in the Petrashevsky Circle, a radical organization active in Russia in 1847–48. Petya, while sympathetic to Baburin's republican ideals, voices Turgenev's own views in criticizing the efficacy of his methods: revolution, he argues, is impossible in Russia.

The story reaches its conclusion in 1861, as Baburin welcomes the emancipation of the peasants and dies soon afterward. It is symbolic of Turgenev's own disappointment with the results of the emancipation that Baburin, who, like Turgenev, had lived through the dark days of the reign of Nicholas I and into the brighter future initially apparently offered by Alexander II, should die at the very moment when all he had been striving for was theoretically achieved. His dreams of a free Russia, however, die with him.

Most of these stories, it must be admitted, are inferior to Turgenev's previous works. This does not hold, however, for "A King Lear of the Steppes" (1870), written as well and as convincingly as anything he ever published. Turgenev always admired Shakespeare, and once even tried to convert Tolstoy to his opinion. While based loosely on events that had actually occurred on an estate near Spasskoe, the story is nonetheless loosely and intentionally modeled on Shakespeare's tragedy.

"A King Lear of the Steppes" is started by a group of old university students who meet and then hear one of their number relate a story. The narrator, Dmitry Semenovich, recalls the time when, at fifteen, he was living on his mother's estate. The tale's leading personage, introduced in Turgenev's preferred manner by a physical description, is Martin Kharlov, a neighbor of the narrator's mother and a man of gigantic physical stature. He is a hardworking peasant farmer, stern, demanding, and fearsome, but also honest and proud. He lives in what he calls a "mansion," in reality a rather ramshackle manor house, much of which he built with his own hands. When he was forty the narrator's mother arranged to marry him off to a sickly seventeen-year-old orphan who bore him two daughters but died shortly afterward; the little girls were raised in the narrator's home.

Having established Kharlov's character and those of a few minor characters, Turgenev then describes Kharlov's elder daughter, Anna, a cruel woman, her mild-mannered, complaining, and grasping husband, Sletkin, and the younger, unmarried, haughty, and free-spirited daughter Evlampia. Both the daughters are physically very attractive. Thus in a few short chapters the leading characters and the setting for the story are all finely and vividly outlined.

One night Kharlov has a dream that he interprets as a forewarning of his imminent death, and so sets about drawing up a will to divide his estate immediately between his two daughters. Kharlov is confident of his power within his own family and insists his daughters will stand by him even after he gives them their inheritance. But his generosity proves to be foolishness.

From here on Turgenev expands the story. After the legal formalities of drawing up the will have been completed, there is a meal. When it is over, Souvenir, Kharlov's malicious brother-in-law, tells Kharlov that he has been silly in dividing up his property before his death. A sense of inevitability now pervades the story, compounded by Kharlov's continuing preoccupation with death.

After an interruption in the action, the imminent change in Kharlov's life indeed takes place. Sletkin, with Evlampia as his mistress now, has gained complete control of the estate and Kharlov, although still living in the house, is a mere shadow of his former self. Three weeks later Kharlov is dramatically evicted by Sletkin and his daughters, just as Souvenir had predicted, to be given refuge by the narrator's mother. Taunted by Souvenir, Kharlov suddenly climbs onto the roof of his former "mansion" and starts to dismantle it, beam by beam: "They shall not even have a roof over their heads either," he shouts in a frenzy. A vivid passage ends as Kharlov falls to his death, crushed by the roof's central beam.

Fifteen years later the narrator returns to the scene of the tragedy. Sletkin is dead, unmourned. Anna is the same as ever, still attractive but hard, selfish but an extremely efficient manager of the estate. The narrator wonders whether she deserves what he sees as her happiness, saying: "Everything in the world, good or bad, comes to man not through his deserts, but in consequence of some as yet unknown but logical laws which I shall not take upon myself to indicate, though I sometimes fancy I have a dim perception of them."

Rarely one to leave his stories at loose ends, in the final chapter Turgenev describes a fleeting meeting between the narrator and Evlampia, who has become the leader of a dissident religious sect, perhaps out of remorse, though we cannot be certain. True to himself, Turgenev refuses to moralize. "The storyteller fell silent, and we talked a little longer, and then parted, each to his home."

"A King Lear of the Steppes," with no obvious social message, is a chronicle of family discord and human weakness. Powerfully written and accurately detailed, it leaves the reader lamenting for the human condition, for which Turgenev offers no palliative.

"The Torrents of Spring"

Turgenev's writings of the 1870s were not extensive until he began *Virgin Soil*. Perhaps his only work of lasting significance and real literary merit was "The Torrents of Spring," begun in the middle of 1870, completed at the end of the following year, and published in 1872.

The background for the plot was an encounter in Frankfurt in 1841 between Turgenev and an extremely beautiful young girl who rushed out of a tearoom to ask him to help her brother who had just fainted. Unlike his future heroine Gemma, the girl was not Italian but Jewish, and Turgenev himself, unlike Sanin, sensibly left town the same night, before he got further involved.

The themes of this remarkable novella are characteristic ones: the humiliation that love for an unworthy woman can bring with it, the unhappiness caused by the involvement of a weaker man with a stronger woman, the malevolent influence of sexual passion.

As the story opens, the fifty-year-old Dmitry Sanin is returning home from a party while ruminating on the vanity of the world and the uselessness of life. At home he casts his mind back thirty years to 1840 when, on his way from Italy to Russia, he stopped off in Frankfurt. As he passes a pastry shop a beautiful girl, Gemma, rushes out and asks him to help her brother, Emilio, who, she thinks, is on the point of death. When Sanin revives him from what is apparently only a fainting fit, he is welcomed into Gemma's household as Emilio's savior. The impressionable Sanin cancels his plans to return to Russia and before long has fallen hopelessly in love with Gemma, who, however, is engaged to a repulsive German shopkeeper named Klüber.[1] Eventually Sanin and Gemma realize they love each other, Gemma breaks off her engagement to Klüber, and she and Sanin agree to marry.

Turgenev then develops the story's main theme. Just as he is about to return to Russia to sell his estates, Sanin meets an old acquaintance, Polozov, who is married to a wealthy woman of peasant stock and notable physical attractions. Polozov convinces Sanin that his wife will buy his lands, but Polozova decides to seduce Sanin in order to wreck his projected marriage. Turgenev describes Sanin's seduction in some detail, an unusual thing for him. The description of sexual infatuation in this work is the most explicit in the whole of Turgenev's writings, and even he thought he was rather "immoral" in it. As the story ends a degraded Sanin is in the grip of an uncontrollable passion for Polozova. Sanin writes Gemma a despicable and cowardly letter, after which Polozova coldly keeps him for a while in the circle of her numerous admirers before discarding him.

As Leonard Schapiro has pointed out, there is one dominant theme in this fascinating tale: its interpretation of sex as an unconscious force capable of simply overwhelming reason.[2] This theme had emerged earlier in, for example, "A Correspondence," where the hero abandons an honest and self-sacrificing young girl for the physical attractions of a ballerina, but it is more to the fore here as the moving force of the story's action. Turgenev well knew Schopenhauer's notion that sex was a world energy operating outside man's conscious existence, and that love, however ethereal it might seem, is rooted in the sexual impulse alone. If Turgenev believed this, then his view had shifted, for in many of his earlier stories and novels a largely nonerotic love could have very serious and irrational consequences. But he would return to this subject some ten years later, as we shall see.

The Mysterious Tales

After the publication of *Virgin Soil* much of Turgenev's literary output contains an element of the supernatural, or at least the mysterious. This was by no means a new departure for him, but in the earlier stories the supernatural was but an element, whereas in the later ones it is central to the action.

An interesting factor about most of these stories—usually told by a far-from-omniscient narrator—is that the strange events can be given a rational explanation even if Turgenev does not directly suggest one.[3]

Turgenev's two stories of 1877 provide good examples of this change in emphasis: "Son" ("The Dream") and "Rasskaz ottsa Alekseya" ("The Story of Father Alexis"). Both based on actual, or reported, events, they have a realistically convincing setting, which, some critics argue, diminishes their potential horror. But unlike E. T. A. Hoffmann or Gogol, Turgenev could never invent convincing stories of pure imagination. The young narrator of "The Dream" cannot fathom the strange events he describes, but the older reader can suggest plausible explanations for the mysterious combination of dream, coincidence, illness, fear, death—and the apparent disappearance of a corpse. Yet any explanation remains only a possibility. The supernatural element in "Father Alexis" is less mysterious but rather more frightening. The son of a priest begins his education in a seminary but then decides to go to university, abandoning the religious life. On his first visit home his parents find him a different person: he thinks he is possessed by the devil. During Holy Communion he sees a vision of the devil telling him to spit out the bread, which he does. Convinced that he is condemned to eternal damnation, he loses his sanity and soon dies. Turgenev could have written the story in a sensational manner, but instead relates it calmly, simply, and compassionately.

Arguably the best of these stories—and also more interesting in that they elaborate on some of the themes that had appeared in previous works—are "Pesn' torzhestvuyushchey lyubvi" ("Song of Triumphant Love"), published in 1881, and "Klara Milich" (1882). Dedicated to the memory of his friend Flaubert, and in style recalling the latter's *Legends*, "Song of Triumphant Love" is set in sixteenth-century Ferrara. Two friends, Mucius and Fabius, both handsome, rich, cultured, and artistically talented, fall in love with the beautiful Valeria, who must choose between them. Aided and abetted by her mother, Valeria chooses Fabius, where upon Mucius leaves, promising not to return until his love is a thing of the past. Valeria and Fabius marry and enjoy five years of complete happiness, spoilt only by their inability to have children. Then Mucius returns and settles nearby, with a very mysterious Malay servant. He also brings exotic oriental objects, including an Indian violin on which he plays an exultant melody describing the triumphant feelings caused by satisfied love. The effect of the music on Valeria is striking. Visions of Mucius haunt her by day, he appears in her dreams at night, and various nocturnal meetings apparently occur between them. Fabius stabs Mucius and believes he has killed him, but, revived by the Malay servant, he leaves the house never to return. One day, as Valeria is sitting at the organ, suddenly, as if of their own accord, the notes of the song of triumphant love burst forth. At this moment, for the first time, she feels the stirrings of new life within her womb. And there the story intriguingly ends.

Turgenev was a past master at describing the disturbing but nonetheless uplifting effects of human love, but never before, not even in "The Torrents of Spring," had he written so vividly about an inability to cope with the impulses of a sexual passion, when the erotic appears as a profanation of sacred love.

This idea is further developed in "Klara Milich," now subtitled "After Death." It is based on an actual occurrence, when an actress had committed suicide for unknown reasons by taking poison during a performance. An acquaintance of Turgenev's either saw her act and fell in love with her or else, according to some reports, conceived a passion for her only after her death; in any case his love led to serious mental illness. When he heard the story Turgenev thought it would make "a semifantastic tale in the manner of Edgar Allan Poe."

As in real life, Turgenev's heroine commits suicide by taking poison on stage. Aratov, his unfortunate hero, lives shut off from the world with an old aunt. A friend persuades him to go to a concert where an actress and singer named Klara Milich will appear. At that performance Klara transfixes him with her hypnotic gaze, and soon afterward he receives an unsigned letter, which he guesses is from Klara, suggesting they meet. When they do Klara cannot put her emotions into words, and he does not know how to help her. A little later he reads in a newspaper of her suicide, caused, the report suggests, by an unhappy love affair. Aratov visits a provincial town to see her family, and learns from Klara's diary of her love for him.

From this moment on Aratov becomes obsessed with Klara, who haunts him in dreams and hallucinations. His health begins to suffer. He hears her voice during the nights; she appears before him, seductively, in his bedroom. On another occasion they kiss, and he senses her moist lips and the burning nearness of her body. "Not even Romeo and Juliet," he muses, "ever exchanged a kiss like that. But next time I shall be stronger . . . I shall possess her." The next time she appears to him, he throws himself upon her with the words "You have conquered me . . . Take me. . . ." His aunt discovers him on his knees with his head resting on the armchair where "Klara" had been sitting. A few days later he dies happily, deliriously declaring that he is Romeo who has just taken poison.

Turgenev's view that love is an illness, or even a poison, that destroys people's equilibrium and prevents them from thinking and behaving normally runs consistently through his fiction. So too does the notion that love leads in one form or another to death. That love should still have the same effect from beyond the grave is something new. And yet so finely is "Klara Milich" constructed and related, so convincingly are the characters, especially Aratov, drawn, that the reader believes in at least the possibility of a passion that can survive death.

Prose Poems

Prose Poems, a collection of miniatures written mostly from 1877 to 1879, at their best display Turgenev's art to perfection. Of a total of eighty-three, varying in length from a few lines to a couple of pages, only fifty were published during his lifetime, in 1882. They reflect his preoccupations, most of them quite personal. A number of them deal with death, usually his own, and his abiding fear of it. In 1876 he had written to his friend Yakov Polonsky that his observations of the previous year had convinced him that depression, melancholy, and hypochondria are all nothing but the fear of death, a fear that must increase with every passing year. On 17 March 1877 he wrote that his spirits were darker than the darkness of night. He felt as if the grave were waiting to swallow him up as the days flew past like brief moments. He saw nothing more to do, nothing to hope for, not even anything to wish for. Along with the fear of death *Prose Poems* also show regret for his lost youth and for that of Pauline Viardot. Two extremely moving passages refer to her. One reminds her of the beauty she personifies and which provides the only human immortality possible, while the other asks her not to visit his grave but quietly to read one of their favorite books and to think of him.

Other poems advance two ideas to which Turgenev adhered throughout his life. The first is that nature is an indifferent, impersonal force concerned only with procreation and the survival of all species, and consequently oblivious to human dreams and aspirations. The second theme is the supreme importance of love in human relationships: "Love, I thought, is stronger than death and the fear of death. Only through it, through love, does life continue and progress."

There are poems describing the Russian peasants' experience of continuous hardship and their patience in the face of injustice and imposed disaster. Other pieces have a historical background. The most famous of them, "The Threshold," was suggested by the trial of the revolutionary Vera Zasulich and was first printed illegally at the time of Turgenev's funeral by a clandestine organization, the People's Will. It describes a young girl being questioned before she joins the revolutionary cause. Asked whether she is prepared for the self-denial such a life requires, she affirms she is. Would she commit a crime for the cause? Yes, she is prepared for that too. Then, as she crosses the threshold, one voice cries out "Fool!" while another replies "Saint!" These works include reminiscences of events in Turgenev's life and of his thoughts and emotions aroused when, for example, he bade farewell to the dying Nekrasov. There are bitter satires displaying a hatred one does not expect of Turgenev. And finally there are nightmares, full of despair at the futility of life.

While *Prose Poems*—which Turgenev originally did not intend to publish because they were too personal—are not all of the same high quality, at least the best of them offer valuable insights into his most intimate thoughts. Like the best of his fiction, they contain not a single wrong word, not a single superfluous one. With a few brief strokes of his literary brush he expresses what he wants to say brilliantly and succinctly. The poems were, he wrote, his farewell to literature.[4] That farewell was sad, but it was also dignified, and beautifully worded.

Fragments from Reminiscences

The two short stories "Starye portrety" ("Old Portraits") and "Otchayanny" ("A Desperate Character") were published under the general title *Otryvki iz vospominaniy—svoikh i chuzhikh* (*Fragments from Reminiscences—My Own and Others'*). While he was working on the former Turgenev apparently intended to write a new series of stories recalling *A Sportsman's Sketches*, which, it will be remembered, had grown out of the initial success of "Khor and Kalinych." He wrote to Annenkov on 22 November 1880: "It would be a miracle if 'Old Portraits' were also to prove as fruitful." Unfortunately the miracle did not occur. "Old Portraits" appeared in 1881 in the liberal newspaper *Poryadok* (*Order*), edited by Turgenev's publisher of that time, Mikhail Stasyulevich, and "A Desperate Character" in the *Messenger of Europe* at the beginning of the following year. Neither of them ranks among Turgenev's best stories but both have their virtues and were relatively successful with the Russian critics upon publication and even more so abroad when translated into French and English.

In both stories Turgenev is in a nostalgic mood and unconcerned with contemporary problems. He also reverts to a style in which he had earlier proved himself a master, that of portraiture. Both are first-person narratives, although "A Desperate Character" is removed a stage when Turgenev has one member of a group relate the tale. Although both stories are clearly related to Turgenev's own experiences, in his preface to the first edition he declared "that I chose the first-person narrative form for my own convenience and so I ask the reader not to take the 'I' of the narrator exactly for the 'I' of the author. This is implied by the title of the fragments: 'Reminiscences—my own and *others*.'" The ones by the "others," however, were never written.

"Old Portraits" takes place "many years ago," in the 1830s, during the reign of Nicholas I, well before serfdom was abolished. It relates the story of Aleksey Sergeich Telegin, based on one of Turgenev's uncles, and his wife Malanya. They live a quiet, almost elegiac life in a typical manor house of the steppes, spacious but unostentatious. The only notable thing it contains is an immense collection of paintings. The house is ringed with office buildings, peasant huts, and a modest orchard, and the whole estate is set amid ten miles of empty steppe: "No lofty object met the eye; not a tree, not even a belfry," the narrator writes. Telegin is as apparently old-fashioned and at peace with the world as are the surroundings in which he lives. A conservative who believes that things have grown steadily worse since the death of Catherine the Great at the end of the previous century (he was born in 1760), Telegin is a religious man, and also well-read, at least in Russian literature published before 1800. Telegin's wife, Malanya, a former beauty, "the Moscow Venus," is devout and kind-hearted, but a rather empty-headed chatterbox.

Both Telegin and his wife die within a few months of each other in 1848, a year that sees the end of the idyllic pastoral Turgenev has been painting. But he concludes the story with a description of a happening that contrasts sharply with the charming picture of life on a typical country estate, and points up the darker side of serfdom to an extent far beyond anything found in *A Sportsman's Sketches*. When the narrator makes his final visit to the Telegin estate, one of Telegin's serfs comes to him in utter despair. It transpires that one of Telegin's neighbors, a man known for his brutality toward his serfs, has discovered that the man really belongs to him, and demands his immediate return. The kind-hearted Telegin offers him rather more money for the serf than is strictly necessary in such circumstances, but the neighbor refuses any monetary settlement. The serf, dreading his fate, threatens to kill his new owner rather than submit. Indeed, a bit later he does just that, and is sentenced to the mines for life. Turgenev's portrayal of the arbitrary nature of serfdom as an institution had never been clearer, not even in "Mumu." And yet, just as before, he leaves the story to speak for itself, with no explicit comment.

Annenkov told Turgenev, when the latter submitted "Old Portraits" to him for advice, that the serf should commit suicide as a form of protest against such inhumane treatment. But Turgenev rejected such a conclusion, for he believed peasants did not normally behave in that way. He understood that in adverse circumstances the Russian peasant normally accepted with fortitude whatever life offered him.

"A Desperate Character" portrays a disillusioned and rootless member of the Russian minor nobility. The outcome is a faithful picture of one of Turgenev's first cousins, Mikhail Alekseevich Turgenev, whom Turgenev had earlier described in a letter to Annenkov of 12 October 1860 as follows: "That crazy good-for-nothing who was nicknamed Shamil in the province had at one time a very decent estate, and then became a monk, a gypsy, and an army officer, and would now appear to have dedicated himself to the profession of drunkard and cadger. I have written to my uncle and asked him to support this dissolute buffoon at Spasskoe."

As the story opens, a group of eight people are discussing contemporary events. One remarks that he cannot understand men these days: there has never been anything like such desperate fellows before. The narrator of the story disagrees and relates the tale of his nephew, or rather cousin, Misha Poltev. Born in 1828 and brought up by his kindly yet strict, old-fashioned, limited, and religious parents, Misha was, until their deaths when he was eighteen, an obedient and even rather effeminate, young boy. Then a remarkable change occurs.

The next time the narrator sees Misha he discovers that he has sold the family estates for a trifling sum, dresses somewhat unusually, and spends his money on drink, horses, and riotous living among a band of gypsies. A few months later he turns up looking like an itinerant pilgrim and proclaiming that as he has now spent every penny he is going off to become a monk and seek atonement. He begins to write letters begging for forgiveness and asking for help, usually financial. A month or two later the narrator hears that Misha has become a junior officer in the Caucasus, but he turns out to be less than useless as an officer.

Misha later attributes his unpredictable behavior to wretchedness. "If one comes to oneself, begins to feel, to think of the poverty and injustice in Russia," he says, "Well, it's all over . . . one is so wretched—one wants to put a bullet through one's head. . . . One's forced to start drinking." Misha was also a passionate gambler, and upon being discharged from the army, he takes to a life of debauchery and joins a gang of drunken itinerant beggars. The narrator offers him a home if he will give up his heavy drinking, and Misha, in a fit of self-pity, accepts. His reformation does not last long. He grows wild and morose, and cannot stand the ordered way of life of the narrator's country estate, and so departs to resume his former ways. Later on he marries and tries to settle down, but is overcome by feelings of guilt and inadequacy, and soon dies. "He embodied," concludes the narrator, "a thirst for self-destruction, wretchedness, dissatisfaction. . . ."

Is Poltev little more than the last in a long line of memorable "superfluous men"? Or was Turgenev trying to make some comment about the people of the late 1870s, as many thought? In a letter of January 1882 Turgenev explained that he had tried to portray a type of person he knew from his own youth but who exhibited remarkable similarities with some contemporary young people. He was consequently criticized for maligning contemporary youth just as he had been some twenty years in connection with *Fathers and Sons*. This naturally upset him, yet he still believed that the youth of the time *were* the same type as his desperate character. Social conditions had changed, but there was still, he said, "the same recklessness, the same restlessness, the same lack of will, and the same vagueness and indeterminateness in what they are demanding." Turgenev offers no explanation for the strange personality of Poltev, but he recognizes the frightful waste that his life amounts to.

Chapter Eight
Turgenev's Letters

Most well-known Russian writers of the nineteenth century tried their hands at different literary genres. While Pushkin and Lermontov are best remembered for their poetry, they both wrote plays, a novel (albeit Pushkin's *Eugene Onegin* is in verse), and shorter prose works; Gogol and Tolstoy published short stories, plays, and novels; Chekhov began his literary career with brief humorous "anecdotes" before progressing through stories to plays; and Dostoyevski produced short stories and novels. Turgenev was the most versatile of them all, publishing poetry, plays, novellas, short stories, and novels. Moreover, most of these authors were also inveterate letter writers. If Tolstoy was the most prolific author in this area, Turgenev was the most stylish and accomplished. If his stories and novels have been criticized for concentrating on contemporary social problems, or conversely, for not doing so, or his characterization and plotting thought limited, his style has always been regarded as exceptional. And that reputation has survived. His language has always been thought of as exemplary, even by as recent a writer as Solzhenitsyn, with whom he has little else in common. The narrator of Solzhenitsyn's "Matryona's Home," while wandering around the countryside looking for "the old Russia," the Russia of *A Sportsman's Sketches* perhaps, and noting the names given to the new collective farms, names such as Peatproduce, exclaims: "Oh Turgenev, if you had been living now!"

While Turgenev's letters do not display the same meticulous attention to style and detail as his fictional works, they demonstrate his writing ability just as amply. Errors in spelling or grammar (no matter in what language he was writing) and clumsiness of expression are as rare in Turgenev as they are common in Tolstoy. While he always composed his fiction in Russian—and could not comprehend how anyone could write convincingly in a language other than his mother tongue—he corresponded with non-Russians in French, German, or English, and the lofty standard he attained in especially the first two belies his own opinion. There is the same stylish exposition, the same mastery of the language, the same feeling for it. An early German publisher of his German correspondence with Ludwig Pietsch claimed that Turgenev's description of a very cold winter day in Weimar was unsurpassed in the whole of German literature. One of Turgenev's correspondents complained that he wrote so well as to call the sincerity of what he was saying into question. One can only sympathize with the unfortuate Turgenev: he was constantly criticized, even for his virtues.

Nearly 7,000 of Turgenev's letters have been published; many more have been withheld for various reasons or have not come to light. They cover a period of more than fifty years, from those of the twelve-year-old boy in 1831 to his favorite uncle (none of his letters to either of his parents has survived) until almost the day of his death in 1883. Comparatively few survive from his earlier days, and there are only about 150 before 1850, but after that almost every year sees an increase. His mother complained that he hardly ever wrote to her when he was a young man, and concluded that he was as lazy as a correspondent as he was in other aspects of his life. After he had taken up more or less permanent residence abroad because of his lifelong affection for Pauline Viardot, he would write to Russia, as he told Marko Vovchok in 1859, "in order to receive replies." He had condemned himself "to the life of a gypsy" and had "given up all thought of a family life." Through the replies he hoped to receive he could keep in touch with the Russia he loved. He also missed speaking Russian, and correspondence substituted for that.

Much of Turgenev's correspondence is naturally ephemeral, consisting of arrangements and appointments (or apologies for having missed them), day-to-day trivia, thanks for invitations, letters of recommendation, and business matters having to do with his estates in Russia and his writing and publishing at home and abroad (in these latter matters he was meticulous to a fault).

Turgenev liked, as he often remarked, to carry on conversations by post. His correspondence with Annenkov is a fascinating literary discussion; many of his letters to his friends Afanasy Fet aand Vasily Botkin are lighthearted, yet set forth his views on a multitude of subjects. He also enjoyed arguing by letter, not only about literature but also on social and political matters. His letters to Alexander Herzen and Mikhail Saltykov-Shchedrin, for example, show him to be more politically aware and realistic than the usual conception of him as a vacillating liberal might suggest.

Turgenev was always willing to help young writers (and he considered anyone born later than he to be "young"). If he thought their writings worthwhile he would say so and encourage them, but he never hesitated to say so if he thought them untalented or affected. He would also suggest how their works might be improved. It is from such letters too that his own literary criteria can be gleaned.

Of Turgenev's 589 known correspondents, 149 were women. With them he was charming and considerate—and on occasion flirtatious. He apparently felt easier in discussing the emotional side of life with women, while venting his anger and frustration to his male correspondents, especially his friend Ivan Borisov. It is not surprising that his numerous letters to Pauline Viardot are a little more circumspect: they are rather like a diary of his life, with comments on what he had been doing, whom he had met, what he had seen. The only woman for whom he showed scant affection was his illegitimate daughter Paulinette. He was often ill-tempered over what he considered her bad behavior and abrasive about her actions. He saw it as his paternal duty to provide for her materially as best he could, but nothing more.

All in all, Turgenev's letters reflect the many sides of his life, both private and literary; they point to the different aspects and difficulties of writing; they contain his opinions on the literary, social, and political events of his time, both in Russia and in Western Europe. They display a marvelous vivacity, a sharp intelligence, and a lively (and on occasion malicious) sense of humor. Like his works of fiction, his letters display the same powers of observation and evocation, contain the same lyrical descriptions of the wonders of nature—indeed, there are passages in his correspondence as good as anything he ever wrote—and they exhibit the same reluctance to judge, to moralize, or to preach.

A central impression of Turgenev the man that one obtains from his letters is that he had a great lack of self-confidence. If others think him successful, or it becomes obvious, even to him, that he is famous, he is still slow to be convinced. Never did he rank himself among the great masters of literature, those whom he read, reread, and admired—Pushkin, Gogol, Goethe, not to mention Shakespeare or Molière. He told Annenkov as early as 1852 that one could not compare the "free, swift brushstrokes" of those natural geniuses with "the thin squeaking of his own pen." Great writers create in wholesale fashion, he said, while he sat in a retail shop providing day-to-day fare. While always grateful for favorable comments on his work, he was never entirely persuaded, and he usually agreed with those who found him wanting. He nonetheless appreciated, and indeed needed, the support of stronger characters than he: Belinsky, Annenkov, Pauline Viardot, Flaubert, even Tolstoy, when they were still on speaking terms. When *A Sportsman's Sketches* encountered enthusiastic acclaim, he was pleased that the left-wing intelligentsia liked the book and proud when it was suggested to him that it had helped prepare the ground for the abolition of serfdom, and yet some time later he told Annenkov that he had recently reread it, and "parts of [the series] are pallid, fragmentary . . . some parts are oversalted and others undercooked." But there were some true notes that would save the whole book. *Rudin*, he told the critic Alexander Druzhinin in 1855, would demonstrate that he was finished as a writer. Rarely would he defend himself unless provoked, as during his contretemps with Goncharov, who had commented adversely on *Home of the Gentry*. "What would you have me do?" he wrote in 1859. "I don't want to give up writing. I am left with composing stories where, without pretending that my characters are either complete or strong or that I have penetrated life to any great depth . . . I could write what came into my head. . . . Whatever I might want to write, what emerges is only a series of sketches."

Turgenev reacted in a similar way to the hostile reception of *Fathers and Sons*. While he was surprised that Dostoyevski liked it and delighted at the strong support he received from the left-wing critic Dmitry Pisarev (who probably saw himself in Bazarov), his letters of that time and later show he felt extremely hurt by the attacks on his book. *Smoke* was even worse. He admitted shaking like a leaf when he read the reviews, and the almost universal condemnation of *Virgin Soil* convinced him "in his heart of hearts" that he was a failure. The whole thing, he told his brother, was a fiasco.

Turgenev thought of himself as a writer during some sort of interregnum between Gogol and whoever was to succeed him. Such moods explain his frequent pledges to abandon writing altogether, his assertions that he was finished, that he lacked true creative power. From this stems the mood of nostalgia that permeates much of his writing after *Fathers and Sons* and that is reflected in his letters, and reinforced by melancholy complaints about his health and a sense of resignation in the face of death.

One of the more striking facts to emerge from a reading of Turgenev's letters is that he held certain social and political views consistently throughout his life. He might have dithered and withdrawn from the struggle when faced with vehement opposition, but he was always a moderate: he hated fanaticism and supported human rights. He was convinced that only compromise or gradual change could succeed. War and revolution were futile. It was frequently brought home to him that such views upset both his friends and his enemies, but this did not deter him. When Léon Gambetta was elected in France Turgenev compared that country favorably to Russia. "You might think me an optimist," he wrote to Saltykov-Shchedrin in February 1876, "but it is a long time since I have looked to the future with such confidence; I still have greater hopes for France than I do for Russia, which seems to me to be sinking daily ever further into a sort of foul-tasting blancmange." During the Franco-Prussian War he had told Annenkov that the Germans were amazed by their success: "From the very beginning, as you know, I was wholeheartedly on their side, for I see the complete downfall of Napoleon's empire as the salvation of civilization and as something that would make possible the untrammeled development of free institutions in Europe." Turgenev disliked systems and dogma. He lacked religious faith, and hated most of all what he saw as the all-embracing vision of Roman Catholicism, which stifled man's ability to think for himself. He was for those who protested, he told Pauline Viardot, for "Prometheus, Satan, revolt, individuality." He wanted truth, not salvation, and expected to find it through reason, not grace.

He applied these views to Russia's problems in particular during his long epistolary arguments with Herzen, writing from Paris in November 1862:

Enemy of mysticism and absolution, you mystically bow down before the Russian sheepskin coat and see in it the great abundance, innovation, and originality of future social forms. . . . History, philology, statistics all means nothing to you. Facts mean nothing to you, even the undoubted fact that we Russians belong by language and by birth to the European family . . . and consequently . . . must travel the same road. . . . [You] attack everything that should be dear to every European and consequently us too—civilization, legality, and finally the revolution itself—and having filled the heads of the young with your half-fermented socio-Slavophile views, you send them out intoxicated and befuddled into a world where they will stumble at the first step.

Turgenev has been criticized for his faith in Western-style liberalism, but was he any more in error than Herzen, Tolstoy, or Chernyshevsky?

The letters display another of Turgenev's traits: his ability to fall out with friends. The editors Nekrasov, Katkov, Chernyshevsky, and Dobrolyubov all aroused his displeasure. So did his fellow writers Goncharov and Dostoyevski. But most revealing of all was his tentative friendship, followed by a seventeen-year quarrel, with Tolstoy. More than anything else Turgenev valued beauty and art, things that Tolstoy increasingly distrusted. Paradoxically, in the late 1850s Tolstoy had suggested that Russia needed a new journal devoted to aesthetic questions, and Turgenev had upbraided him for discounting social problems. It is not "lyrical twittering that the times are calling for, nor birds singing on boughs. . . . You loathe politics, and it is indeed a dirty, dusty, low business, yet there is dirt and dust in the streets, and yet we cannot do without towns." That was, though, a passing phase, particularly with Tolstoy. Turgenev always sensed an inexplicable gulf between him and Tolstoy, but he recognized his genius from the beginning and urged his friends to read his novels. Tolstoy, on the other hand, could not stand Turgenev, and the break between them seemed inevitable. Turgenev's disparaging remarks about Tolstoy's great novels do not spring from any envy for the man he regarded as the greatest living novelist, but rather from conviction that he had lost his way or was deceiving the reader. He found the early parts of *War and Peace* "positively bad, tedious, and unsuccessful," cold and dull, focused too much on unnecessary details. In 1868 he wrote to Annenkov that he found many of Tolstoy's pages quite marvelous: the hunt, the sleigh-ride at night, etc., indeed all the domestic and descriptive passages. "But the historical addition," he declared, "with which his readers are particularly delighted, is a puppet comedy and charlatanism." There are pages in *War and Peace* that would live as long as Russian literature, but there was not a trace of any real picture of the period, no development of character, only a huge amount of "that old psychological stuff."

When *Anna Karenina* appeared Turgenev was even more severe in his criticism. He praised what he found to be excellent in the novel, but it still contained much that was tedious. "It is all due to Moscow, the Slavophile gentry class, the Orthodox, old maids," he said. He told Baroness Vrevskaya in 1876 that Tolstoy could not get out of "the Moscow bog . . . Orthodoxy, the gentry, the Slavophiles, gossip, ignorance, self-importance, the officer in him, the little lord of the manor," and so on. Turgenev bemoaned the fact that such a gifted man would perish in the chaos he himself had created— "but then that is always happening in Russia!"

On the other hand, what really upset Tolstoy about Turgenev had little to do with his writing, which he thought sincere and well done, even if lacking in any serious content. It was Turgenev the man, a talented individual who wasted his gifts on trivialities, who angered him. Their correspondence shows that there were very limited grounds for friendship between them.

When all the contemporary problems Turgenev discusses have faded into the past, he retains his wonderful ability to describe the natural word. It emerges in many of his letters, especially some to Pauline Viardot describing his various shooting trips. Nature is a source of delight to him even though he regards it as nothing more than a biological process. He adores the beauty of nature but not the "greedy, egotistical power" of nature that creates the stars above but also the warts on his skin, that allows the nightingale to pour forth its marvelous song as it crushes some wretched insect in its claw. What he means is well expressed in a letter to Pauline Viardot of April 1848, written after he had been out alone in a forest near Paris:

I spent more than four hours in the forest, sad, moved, attentive; absorbed in and absorbing what I saw. The impression made by nature on a man when he is alone is a strange one. There is something in it of the *fresh* sadness which is in all the smells of the fields, a little of the *serene* melancholy in the singing of the birds. . . . Ah, I cannot bear the sky; but life and reality, with all its capriciousness and dangers, with all its customs and fleeting beauty—I adore it all. Speaking personally, I am attached to the ground. I would prefer to watch the precipitous movements of the damp foot of a duck as it scratches the back of its head by the side of a lake, or the long sparkling drops of water falling slowly from the mouth of a cow as it stands motionless and up to its knees drinking water from a pond, to anything the cherubims . . . could perceive in their heavens.

Then Turgenev apologizes for being in a "philosophic-pantheistic mood." But self-mockery is not the least endearing facet of his personality to shine through his varied and fascinating correspondence.

Chapter Nine
Looking Back

For a decade or so in the middle of the nineteenth century Turgenev was the best known, most widely read, and most controversial writer in Russia, and later he became the first Russian novelist to achieve international recognition. Literary tastes, however, change constantly, and Turgenev's reputation fluctuated almost from the very beginning of his career, and fluctuated more than that of any other comparable Russian writer. While he has always had his admirers, he has also enjoyed more than his fair share of detractors.

When discussing Russian writers, critics often use other authors as a yardstick. When this is done with Turgenev, it is usually to his detriment. A typical example would be: "Turgenev painted people of the same epoch, the same generation; he dealt with the same material; he dealt with it as an artist and a poet, as a great artist and poet. But his vision was weak and narrow when compared with that of Tolstoy, and his understanding was cold and shallow compared with that of Dostoevsky. His characters beside those of Tolstoy seem caricatures and beside those of Dostoevsky they are conventional."[1] Similarly, and more sweepingly, the contemporary critic Nikolay Strakhov considered that in the vividness, vitality, and depth of his literary creation Turgenev fell short not only of Tolstoy, Goncharov, and Ostrovsky, but also of Dostoyevski and Pisemsky. He continued: "Perhaps the highest measure which his characters use is the dream of some happiness . . . a happiness that seems to stand before their eyes, but which for the greater part only flickers in the distance, eternally beckoning and eternally vanishing, so that in the end they are left with a life unfulfilled or broken, and the fear of death." But even here Turgenev was not successful, for this motif "does not come out with full force, is not embodied with artistic vividness, but sounds somehow timidly and plaintively."[2] Even critics who praise him seem to do so somewhat grudgingly. Turgenev "might not have dug so deep into human emotion as Dostoevsky or ranged as wide as Tolstoy. Yet he led the way. He gave us beauty and his own healthy judgment which his liberal views did not unbalance. He described honest and sincere people, and kept his sympathy, his charity, and his ideals."[3] More recently it has been suggested that his "exquisitely planned, finely wrought books are 'faded',"[4] the social and political phenomena he described have lost their interest, and he tends toward the sentimental. Further, some say his view of human relations, especially of love between the sexes, is unreal or overly pessimistic, his heroes are weak and vacillating like Turgenev himself, and his heroines idealized. The list of shortcomings can be extended, and it must be admitted that there is justification for all of them. It is quite true that he "cannot boast the verbal exuberance and astounding inventiveness of a Gogol, the profound energy and conviction of a Dostoevsky wrestling with problems of a sort our age thinks very relevant, the epic sweep and inquiry to be found in Tolstoy, the painstaking attention to detail and psychological analysis of a Goncharov."[5] And yet. . . .

Turgenev's best stories are models of construction, and his use of language is superb. In days of doubt, he wrote in *Prose Poems*, in days of weary uncertainty over the fate of his country, the Russian language was his only support. "Oh great, mighty, true, and free Russian language! If it were not for you, I should have fallen into despair at the sight of what is happening in my native land." While he might lack inventiveness and prefer to remain on the surface of things, however brilliant that surface might be, Turgenev is at his best when he keeps things simple, when he describes rather than analyzes. The atmosphere of many of his best stories is nostalgic; he dwells in an idyllic past and regrets his lost youth. He takes no interest in searching psychological analysis, and his plots are never complicated. But there is always a striking musicality, a gentle irony, and a moving lyricism in his prose. His view of man's helplessness in the face of the indifferent forces of nature is not at all encouraging, but he avoids the Romantic Fallacy, and his actual descriptions of nature and the Russian countryside are unsurpassed in their beauty of expression, accuracy of detail, and evocative power. He has a strong feeling for place and time. He loves contrasting characters. He avoids dogma and preaching. "Impartiality and a wish to seek only the Truth are two of the good qualities that I thank nature for having given me," he wrote Alexander Druzhinin in 1856.

Turgenev was never politically active and distrusted those who were, even when they upbraided him for his passivity. He saw himself primarily as a writer but, as he told the czar once, an independent one with a conscience and moderate opinions. He defined himself as a "dynastic" liberal who thought no reforms in Russia possible unless they were decreed from above, and that revolution was quite foreign to Russia's historical traditons. In his novels he examined what he thought significant in contemporary Russia, even though they are all love stories too, and despite their limitations an historian is well advised to look to him for a picture of the development of radical opinion in mid-nineteenth-century Russia and for realistic descriptions of peasant life before the Emancipation.

Turgenev once said that he was first and foremost a realist, interested more than anything else in "the living truth of the human physiognomy." This provides a clue to the strengths of his methods of characterization and his writing style in general. Although he frequently discusses ideas, he never takes the ideas themselves as his starting point. He finds a suitable character first, and then filters the ideas through that creation. Nearly all his leading characters, though, are limited in one way or another, not least by Turgenev's own philosophical pessimism. He believed lofty human aspirations to be rarely realizable, viewed individual men and women as insignificant and their actions as restricted by their own natures and by fate. These convictions are paralleled by his view that love is transitory and apparently inseparable from death, that it is an illness, a poison, or a madness, leading to uncontrollable and irrational behavior on the part of those who experience it. Yet as Richard Freeborn reminds us, in his greatest works Turgenev compensates for this by achieving a subtle balance between the poles of human experience—between love and death, joy and sadness, youth and age, innocence and maturity. From this balance emerge the momentary harmony, the momentary unity between hero and heroine, the momentary promise of happiness, though happiness itself merely serves to underline the fact of life's tragicomic impermanence.[6]

Turgenev's star may have dimmed over the years, but it will never be extinguished altogether. *A Sportsman's Sketches*, his heroes Rudin and Bazarov, a marvelous succession of heroines, *A Month in the Country*, "First Love," and "The Torrents of Spring," and some of his short stories will continue to fascinate, delight, and even infuriate readers. And through his writings memories of Turgenev the man will live on also. "Every gift has been heaped on his cradle," Joseph Conrad once wrote of him. "Absolute sanity and the deepest sensibility, the clearest vision and the quickest responsiveness, penetrating insight and unfailing generosity of judgment, an exquisite perception of the visible world and an unerring instinct for the significant, for the essential in the life of men and women, the clearest mind, the warmest heart, the largest sympathy—and all that in perfect measure."[7] Not for nothing did Henry James call Turgenev "the beautiful genius."

Notes and References

Chapter One

1. Ivan Turgenev, *Polnoe sobranie sochinenii i pisem* (*Collected Works and Letters*) (Moscow, 1960–68), 1:408.
2. Included in the report, probably by M. I. Semevskii, "I. S. Turgenev na vechernei besede 4-go marta 1880 god" (Turgenev at an evening conversation on the 4th March 1880), *Russkaia starina* (*Russian Antiquity*) 11 (1883):201–16.
3. *Polnoe sobranie*, 15:232.
4. Ibid, 14:8–9.
5. Alexandre Zviguilsky, *Ivan Tourguénev: Nouvelle correspondance inédite* (*New Unpublished Letters*) (Paris, 1972), 1:355.
6. See also his poem "Kroket v Vindzore" ("Croquet at Windsor").

Chapter Two

1. Richard Freeborn, *Turgenev: The Novelist's Novelist* (Oxford, 1963), 25.
2. D. S. Mirsky, *A History of Russian Literature* (London: Routledge & Kegan Paul, 1949), 140.
3. See, for example, Victor Ripp, *Turgenev's Russia* (Ithaca, N.Y.: Cornell University Press, 1980), 26.
4. I am indebted to T. A. Greenan and Sir Isaiah Berlin for their helpful comments and information. See the former's edition of the Russian text, *Mesiats v derevne* (Letchworth: Bradda, 1971), 1–14, and the latter's introduction to his translation entitled *A Month in the Country* (Harmondsworth: Penguin Books, 1981), 7–17.

Chapter Three

1. Lord David Cecil in his introduction to Sir Isaiah Berlin's translation of *First Love* (London, 1965), 12.

Chapter Four

1. Notably a plan discovered amongst Turgenev's papers. See also the chapter on Turgenev's exile in 1852–53 in Nikolai Gur'iar, *Ivan Sergeevich Turgenev* (Iur'ev: K. Mattisen, 1907), 157.
2. Freeborn, *Turgenev*, 41.
3. Ripp, *Turgenev's Russia*, 29–30.

4. Quoted in Ian Grey, *The Romanovs* (Garden City, N.Y.: Doubleday, 1970), 289.

5. For a discussion of Turgenev's complicated relationship with the *Contemporary* see particularly Mikhail Izmailov, *Turgenev i krug "Sovremennika"* (*Turgenev and the "Contemporary" Circle*) (Moscow: Academia, 1930).

6. For a fascinating and stimulating comparison of Onegin, Pechorin, and Rudin see Frank Seeley, "The Heyday of the 'Superfluous Man' in Russia," *Slavonic and East European Review* 31 (1952–53):92–112.

Chapter Five

1. Rosemary Edmonds, introduction to her translation (Harmondsworth, 1965), 10.

2. David Lowe, *Turgenev's "Fathers and Sons"* (Ann Arbor: University of Michigan Press, 1983), 16–17.

3. Sir Isaiah Berlin, *Fathers and Children* (Oxford, 1972), 37–38.

Chapter Six

1. Edward Garnett, *Turgenev: A Study* (London, 1917), 133–34.

2. Freeborn, *Turgenev*, 157.

3. Mirsky, *History of Russian Literature*, 195.

4. Freeborn, *Turgenev*, 162.

Chapter Seven

1. Turgenev was accused of being prejudiced against the Germans in "The Torrents of Spring," and throughout the story he has not a good word to say about them. Probably influenced by what he considered the unnecessarily harsh treatment the Germans gave the defeated French at the end of the Franco-Prussian War, Turgenev was not disposed to counter such accusations except by saying that he had been even harder on his own countrymen many times in the past.

2. Leonard Schapiro, *Turgenev: His Life and Times* (Oxford, 1978), 251–52.

3. For an interesting discussion of these "mysterious" stories see Marina Ledkovsky, *The Other Turgenev: From Romanticism to Symbolism* (Würzburg, 1973), in particular chapter 3.

4. For a somewhat less delicate opinion of the *Prose Poems* see Turgenev's letter to Ludwig Pietsch of 25 December 1882, where he also suggests that they are intended for very few eyes, least of all Russian ones.

Chapter Nine

1. Maurice Baring, *Landmarks in Russian Literature* (1910; reprinted, London: Methuen, 1960), 63.

2. Quoted by Nina Brodiansky, "Turgenev's Short Stories: A Re-evaluation," *Slavonic and East European Review* 32 (1954–54):70.

3. Sir Edmund Spriggs, cited by Nina Brodiansky, *The Harveian Method in Literature* (London, 1945).

4. Charles Moser, *Ivan Turgenev* (New York, 1972), 3, summarizes views of other critics.

5. Ibid.

6. Freeborn, *Turgenev*, 191.

7. Joseph Conrad, letter to Edward Garnett, in the latter's *Turgenev*, ix.

Selected Bibliography

PRIMARY SOURCES

1. Collected works and letters

Ivan Tourguénev: lettres inédites à Pauline Viardot et sa famille (Ivan Turgenev: unpublished letters to Pauline Viardot and her family). Edited by Henri Granjard and Alexandre Zviguilsky. Lausanne: L'Age d'Homme (Age of Man), 1972.

Ivan Tourguénev: nouvelle correspondance inédite (Ivan Turgenev: new unpublished correspondence). Edited by Alexandre Zviguilsky. 2 vols. Paris: Librairie des Cinqs Continents (Five Continents), 1971–72.

Polnoe sobranie sochinenii i pisem v dvatsati vos'mi tomakh (Collected works and letters in twenty-eight volumes). Moscow: Nauka (Science), 1960–68.

Polnoe sobranie sochinenii i pisem v tridtsati tomakh (Collected works and letters in thirty volumes). Moscow: Nauka (Science), 1978–.

Turgenevskii sbornik: Materialy k Polnomu sobraniiu sochinenii i pisem I. S. Turgeneva (A Turgenev miscellany: materials for the *Collected Works*). Edited by Mikhail Alekseev, N. V. Izmailov, and L. N. Nazarova. 5 vols. Moscow: Nauka (Science), 1964–69.

2. Translations

The first translation into English of anything of Turgenev's was "Photographs from Russian Life," published in *Fraser's Magazine for Town and Country* in 1854. The piece is a version of a French rendition of *A Sportsman's Sketches* that had appeared in Paris earlier the same year. Poor translations of *Fathers and Sons* and *Smoke* appeared in 1867 and 1868, a good one of *Home of the Gentry* entitled *Liza* in 1869 (by W. R. S. Ralston), and of *On the Eve* in 1871, *Rudin* in 1873, and *Virgin Soil* in 1878. The first worthy translator of Turgenev was Constance Garnett.

The Novels of Ivan Turgenev. Translated by Constance Garnett. 15 vols. London: Heinemann, 1894–99. Two further volumes were added in 1921.

The Novels and Stories of Ivan Turgeneff. Translated by Isabel Hapgood. 16 vols. New York: Scribner's, 1903–4.

The Vintage Turgenev. 2 vols. New York: Vintage Books, 1960.

Turgenev's Letters. Translated by A. V. Knowles. London: Athlone; New York: Scribner's, 1983.
Turgenev: Letters. Translated by David Lowe. 2 vols. Ann Arbor: Ardis, 1983.

SECONDARY SOURCES

1. Bibliography

Nazarova, L. N., and Alekseev, A. D., comps. *Bibliografiia literatury o I. S. Turgeneve, 1918–67* (Bibliography of literature on I. S. Turgenev 1918–67). Leningrad: Nauka (Science), 1970. Comprehensive list of works published in Russian since the revolution.
Vitberg, F. A., and Modzalevskii, B. I.., comps. *Katalog vystavki v pamiat' Turgeneva v Akademii Nauk* (Catalogue of the exhibition at the Academy of Sciences in memory of Turgenev). St. Petersburg: Izdatel'stvo Imperatorskoi Akademii nauk (Publishing House of the Imperial Academy of Sciences), 1909. Outstanding bibliography of the books exhibited by the Imperial Academy of Sciences to mark the twenty-fifth anniversary of Turgenev's death.
Yachnin, Rissa, and Stam, David, comps. *Turgenev in English: A Checklist of Works by and about Him.* New York: New York Public Library, 1962.
Žekulin, Nicholas, comp. *Turgenev: A Bibliography of Books 1843–1982 By and About Ivan Turgenev.* Calgary: University of Calgary Press, 1985. An impressive compilation; the best English-language bibliography on Turgenev.

2. Biographical and Critical Works

Alekseev, Mikhail, ed. *I. S. Turgenev (1818–1883–1958).* Orel: Orlovskoe knizhnoe izdatel'stvo (Orel Publishing House), 1960. Informative collection of articles and other materials.
Berlin, Isaiah. *Fathers and Children.* Oxford: Clarendon Press, 1972. Excellent summary set against the intellectual ferment of the time.
Bialyi, Grigorii. *Turgenev i russkii realizm* (Turgenev and Russian realism). Moscow: Sovetskii pisatel' (Soviet Writer), 1962. Valuable study of Turgenev's place within the traditions of Russian realism.
Brodskii, N. L. *I. S. Turgenev i russkie sektanty* (Turgenev and the Russian sectarians). Moscow: Nikitinskie subbotniki (Nikitin's Saturday Workers), 1922.
Dubovikov, A. N., and Zil'bershtein, I. S., eds. "Iz Parizhskogo arkhiva I. S. Turgeneva" (From Turgenev's Paris archive). In *Literaturnoe nasledstvo* (Literary heritage). Vol. 73. Moscow: Nauka (Science), 1964.
———, eds. "I. S. Turgenev: Novye materialy i issledovaniia" (I. S. Turgenev: New materials and research). In *Literaturnoe nasledstvo.* Vol. 76. Moscow: Nauka

(Science), 1967. This and the preceding work form an invaluable collection of literary and biographical articles and information.

Fitzlyon, April. *The Price of Genius.* London: Calder, 1964. A life of Pauline Viardot with much of interest on her relations with Turgenev.

Freeborn, Richard. *Turgenev: The Novelist's Novelist.* Oxford: Oxford University Press, 1963. Comprehensive and stimulating study; concentrates on Turgenev's development as a novelist.

Garnett, Edward. *Turgenev: A Study.* London: Collins, 1917. Readable defense of Turgenev against his early critics.

Gershenzon, Mikhail. *Mechta i mysl' I. S. Turgeneva* (Turgenev's dream and thought). Moscow: Tovarishchestvo 'Knigoizdatel'stvo pisatelei v Moskve' (Moscow Writers' Publishing House Cooperative), 1919. A treatment of Turgenev's intellectual development.

Gettmann, Royal. *Turgenev in England and America.* Urbana: University of Illinois Press, 1941. Informative description of Turgenev criticism published in England and America.

Granjard, Henri. *Ivan Tourguénev et les courants politiques et sociaux de son temps* (Ivan Turgenev and the political and social currents of his time). Paris: Institut d'études slaves (Institute of Slavic Studies), 1954. A formidable study, containing useful bibliographies as well.

Kagan-Kans, Eva. *Hamlet and Don Quixote: Turgenev's Ambivalent Vision.* The Hague: Mouton, 1975. An interesting discussion of Turgenev's view of the two poles of the human personality. Drawn principally upon his shorter works.

Kleman, M. K., comp. *Letopis' zhizni i tvorchestva I. S. Turgeneva* (Chronicle of Turgenev's life and work). Moscow: Academia, 1934. Turgenev's life and writings described chronologically.

Ledkovsky, Marina. *The Other Turgenev: From Romanticism to Symbolism.* Würzburg: JAL Verlag, 1973. Concentrates on the shorter works; sees Turgenev in many ways as a precursor of the Russian symbolists.

Lowe, David. *Turgenev's "Fathers and Sons."* Ann Arbor: Ardis, 1983. A detailed and interesting study.

Moser, Charles. *Ivan Turgenev.* New York: Columbia University Press, 1972. Brief but useful and well-written introduction to Turgenev.

Petrova, S. M., and Fridliand, V. G., eds. *I. S. Turgenev v vospominaniiakh sovremennikov* (Turgenev in the memoirs of his contemporaries). 2 vols. Moscow: Khodozhestvennaia literatura (Artistic Literature), 1983. Contributors include Annenkov, Henry James, Kropotkin, and Maupassant.

Poliakova, Liudmila. *Povesti I. S. Turgeneva 70-kh godov* (Turgenev's tales of the 1870s). Kiev: Naukova dumka (Scholarly Thought), 1983. Worthwhile treatment of the later stories, and especially of "Torrents of Spring."

Pritchett, V. S. *The Gentle Barbarian: The Life and Work of Turgenev.* London: Chatto & Windus; New York: Random House, 1977. Many valuable insights into Turgenev's literary manner.

Pustovoit, Petr, *Roman I. S. Turgeneva "Ottsy i deti" i ideinaia bor'ba 60-kh godov XIX veka* (Turgenev's *Fathers and Sons* and the intellectual conflicts of the 1860s). Moscow: Izdatel'stvo moskovskogo universiteta (Moscow University Press), 1960. Detailed and informative survey.

Ripp, Victor. *Turgenev's Russia: From "Notes of a Hunter" to "Fathers and Sons".* Ithaca: Cornell University Press, 1980. Original discussion of *A Sportsman's Sketches*, the first four novels, and the concept of "society."

Schapiro, Leonard. *Turgenev: His Life and Times.* Oxford: Oxford University Press, 1978. A reliable "life" that sets Turgenev's literary achievement against the historical background of his time.

Waddington, Patrick. *Turgenev and England.* London: Macmillan, 1982. Exhaustive and fascinating account of Turgenev's relations with England and the English.

Worrall, Nick. *Nikolai Gogol and Ivan Turgenev.* London: Macmillan, 1982. Discusses and compares the two writers as playwrights.

Yarmolinsky, Avrahm. *Turgenev: The Man—His Art—His Age.* London: Hodder & Stoughton, 1926. A well-written, interesting and readable "life and works."

Index